CHILDS PLAY

A guide to help reclaim and harness your creative power

William Childs

Printed in the United States of America
ISBN: 979-8-218-35073-4

Cover design by William Childs
Cover illustration by Nichole Smith
Interior book design by Sarah Sterner-Hausknecht (sarahsternerdesign.com)
Copy editing by Debbie Burke, Queen Esther Publishing, LLC

First Edition March 2024

For information on speaking opportunities contact William directly at wpchilds1@rcn.com

CHILDS PLAY

To my Mom, who inspired me to dream big.

Prologue:

Many years ago, I noticed that creativity was significantly impacting how I approached my work. It had become a powerful tool that allowed me to do much more than write a catchy headline for an ad or figure out a new marketing campaign. It can also change a person's mindset and reach deep into company's organizational culture.

Creativity is a skill that anyone can master. Too often, we get educated out of our creativity during our formative years only to discover, years later, that you need help finding it again. It's no accident that some of the most successful and well-known brands are among the most creative. You don't have to work at Google, Apple, Pixar, Virgin Group, or Tesla to experience a positive, creative culture; and you certainly don't have to be a creative genius to implement one.

Creative people are often more aware of environments where a toxic leadership approach exists. The best workplace culture is where everyone's skill sets are accepted as instrumental and openly celebrated. Creativity is the catalyst that can help lead that initiative. If you're not sure how or why you should want to bring creativity into your life or company, 'Childs Play' will demonstrate why you should and what skills you'll need to do it.

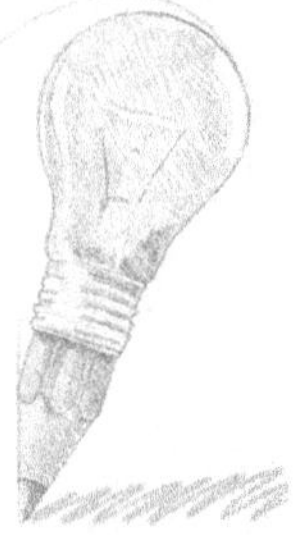

Photo by: Matthew Stenzant

Introduction:

We're all born creative. When we're young, we are at the height of our creative and imaginative powers. Then, as we age, it slowly gets depleted and drained away. Far too many of us go through our lives, never fully realizing our true creative potential. Sir Ken Robinson, an international advisor on education in the arts, said that we don't grow into creativity; we get educated out of it. This book will help anyone rediscover their creative power, the power you knew as a child, the creative energy that today is needed more than ever to help businesses thrive and be innovative. Consider that our world has seen more change in the last hundred years than in the previous million years, and it's easy to see that we have entered what is known as the creative age. After 40 years of working in a wide range of creative roles, I experienced firsthand how creativity is often a much-maligned and misunderstood ideological construct. I spent my career trying to alter that mindset. Finally, I'm ready to share what I've learned. This book aims to shine a light on creativity and how to use it as a dynamic force for change, using real-world examples of how creativity, when used properly, can solve almost any problem it encounters. The book is a guide for anyone who works creatively or manages a creative team. It would also help leaders who need a better understanding of how creative people think and work. More importantly, it will help anyone rediscover their inner genius and show how to apply creativity in both personal and business life. Through the use of real-world situations, in both corporate and small business environments, the stories contained in this book will invigorate and reignite the creative force that lives inside every single one of us.

B. Childs

Table Of Contents:

Section 1: Creativity

Section 2: Creative Leadership

Section 3: Marketing

"Bill Childs is creativity personified. He changed
the way I viewed the importance of creative
in growing our business. He worked with our
sales group and inspired us daily to try harder
to find the best solution for our clients' needs.
He taught us that we should never settle for
"good" solutions because our clients deserve
"great." Our business grew by leaps and
bounds when Bill led our creative team; and
we had a great deal of fun in the process."

Karen Goumakos, General Sales Manager,
Raegan Outdoor

"Bill has been engaging students at DeSales
University for almost 20 years. Students
love his sense of humor, his empathy and
his inspirational messages. Bill encourages
students to take risks with their ideas, and
to think about things in ways they've never
done before. Creative thinking is a key skill
for the future that is often not addressed in
higher education. Bill reminds students that
creativity requires dedication and effort and
tells students to embrace that sometimes
uncomfortable creative side. Bill certainly
embodies all that is creative; he has inspired
students to adapt, innovate and tap in to their
amazing creative potential."

Sue Yacapsin McGorry, Assistant Provost, Assessment
and Student Success at DeSales University

Foreword:

When Bill asked me to write the foreword to Childs Play. Sure, I said, be happy to. Honored, even. I promptly wrote out several paragraphs about all the fun I had working with Bill those many years ago. Sent it to him for approval and then....nothing. Silence... the proverbial pause. Several days passed. Still nothing. Then finally, a call. Not what I was looking for, Childs said. Less about me, more about why creativity is important. Oh. No problem, I said. I'll get right on it.

That was two weeks ago, and I still hadn't nailed it down. I tried writing about the idea of all the world being a stage and how you, as a player, must face your stage fright. Be fearless in your creative endeavors...etc. Nah. Bad idea. Not strong enough. Then I tried writing about how being creative is like being in love. Every time you create, you risk getting your heart broken.

Then it dawned on me. What I am going through, writing this foreword, is what creative people go through all the time. Self-doubt, writer's block, fear of failure. What if people don't like it? For me, being creative is like banging your head against the wall. It only stops hurting when you stop. Not every time I create, but a lot of the time. What always gets me through is knowing that just about everyone who is faced with a creative challenge has gone through the exact same thing. But they do it anyway. Why? Because there is no feeling quite like the rush you get when you know you have created something truly remarkable.

As far as I know, unless you believe in reincarnation, you have one shot, one life. Make the most of it. Be CREATIVE in all your endeavors. Risk failing. Fail and risk again. Learn, love, laugh...and enjoy the ride.   - Dan Ross

Section 1:
Creativity

How can creativity be used as a force for change

and innovation? Can creativity drive new business

revenue? How can it be used to motivate a team,

a division, or an entire company or individual?

How can something that we all inherently have

inside of us be so misunderstood? This section

explores those questions and show why it's time to

give creativity the respect it deserves.

There's no formula to calculate originality.

1

MEDIOCRITY SUCKS

I want nothing to do with mediocrity, and neither should you. I hate that it even exists. To prevent it from creeping into your world, a concerted effort is needed to guard against it permeating your work or personal life. The good news is creativity will always be one of the best tools to fight mediocrity.

I believe that far too many people are content with accepting the status quo. They don't want to make waves or rock the boat. It's easy to be a sheep. The reality is you won't get people excited to work with you if you're content to always just go with the flow. One of the biggest hurdles companies face today is the unwillingness to tackle the tough challenges that could take their business to the next level, and I lay the blame right at the feet of mediocrity. The ability to innovate at a high level is something that runs counter to the thought process of many leaders because they believe the things that made them successful once will work again now as they race toward an uncertain and ever-changing future. Wrong. Wrong. Wrong.

Keith Ferrazzi of Ferrazzi Greenlight, a California-based research consulting firm, believes, *"The choice isn't between success and failure; it's between choosing risk and striving for greatness, or risking nothing and being certain of mediocrity."* Growing up, I was taught that risk and failure were things to be avoided at all costs. In the real world, however, you need both to succeed. Taking calculated risks and failing along the way is how real success is ultimately achieved. Most managers aren't comfortable with employees who fail because of the stigma that's attached to unintended outcomes – that's when mediocrity sets in and the bar gets lowered.

Employees become complacent and less engaged when they feel their ideas are not appreciated or their efforts go unnoticed because they didn't "reach the goal." Be vigilant and pursue excellence anyway.

Albert Einstein, widely regarded as having the twentieth century's most brilliant mind, offered this wisdom *"Great spirits have always encountered violent opposition from mediocre minds. The mediocre mind is incapable of understanding the person who refuses to bow blindly to conventional prejudices and chooses instead to express opinions honestly."* Then there's legendary adman George Lois: *"Only with absolute fearlessness can we slay the dragons of mediocrity that invade our gardens."* Realize that no one sets out to have a mediocre career or average life. But it happens. Don't let it happen to you. Not everyone will understand or participate in your desire to rid the world of mediocrity, and that's okay.

Mediocrity doesn't inspire anyone to go beyond the accepted norms and reach for something better, something extraordinary. I realize that not everyone has the energy required to see it eradicated, and it's often defeating and demoralizing knowing that not everyone shares my disdain for it. However, I will continue to do everything in my power to avoid it and stamp it out. Whatever career, relationship, or situation you may find yourself in, just remember that you always have a choice. And whatever you do, be anything but mediocre.

L E S S O N S
LEARNED

It's never a good sign when a fear of failure overwhelms your ability to take risks.

2

INSPIRATION WILL NOT BE FOUND ON A SPREADSHEET

Today's risk-averse business environments do not support creative thought and ideation the way they should. Most are great at tracking production costs, profitability, taxes, and payroll. Important items that go into running a successful business. But what about creativity?

Adobe recently released a survey looking into creativity around the world. Its "State of Create" global benchmark study surveyed businesspeople in the US, the UK, Germany, France, and Japan. Of those surveyed, 80% felt that unlocking creativity is critical to economic growth.

Also, 75% said they are constantly under pressure to be more creative at work. Therein lies the challenge. If you're feeling pressure to be more creative at work, more than likely, you won't be. Creativity doesn't work like that.

The most shocking stat to me was the one showing that only 39% consider themselves creative.

Clearly, there seems to be a disconnect between the need for more creativity in the workplace and employees not being given the opportunity to do anything about it. Creativity isn't something that can be mandated. You can't order employees to be more creative and then criticize them if results don't show up on your spreadsheet.

Spreadsheets are a window to the past, creativity is a doorway to the future, and any company that embraces, fosters, and nurtures their employees' creativity is going to have to be willing to walk into the unknown.

Our society has done a wonderful job of conditioning us to believe that risk is bad and should be avoided at all costs. Especially when it comes to untested ideas. It's been my experience that most leaders struggle with bringing creativity to their workplace because they are not comfortable with the unpredictable nature that creativity brings with it.

Any untested idea is going to require a leap of faith and involve some risk before it can be turned into a product or new service that can drive revenue. Hugh MacLeod, best-selling author of Ignore Everybody: And 39 Other Keys to Creativity, says that *"Good ideas alter the power balance in relationships. That's why good ideas are initially resisted."*

My favorite quote on this topic comes from Albert Einstein, who was quoted as saying, *"Imagination is more important than knowledge. For knowledge is limited to all we now know and understand, while imagination embraces the entire world, and all there ever will be to know and understand,"* to which he added, *"Logic will get you from point A to B. Imagination will take you everywhere."*

Businesses that are able to tap into that power stand a much better chance of developing new products, unlocking new markets, and driving new revenue streams. Focus on creating an environment for employees to grow and develop creatively and support their efforts by allowing them to take risks. Don't stigmatize mistakes.

The good news is the future only comes one day at a time. The bad news is if you're unwilling to bring creativity into your business, you won't have much of a future to worry about.

LESSONS LEARNED

The road to mastery is riddled with frustration, failure and setbacks. Stay the course.

3

WHAT A SLICE OF PUMPKIN PIE TAUGHT ME ABOUT MASTERING MY CRAFT

Inspiration is everywhere if you are open to it. It may visit you when you least expect it. It happened to me recently at a lunch meeting at a restaurant in King of Prussia, Pennsylvania, called J. Alexander's. I was meeting with Ed Harris, president and CEO of Discover Lancaster and an adjunct professor of marketing strategy at Saint Joseph's University. After we finished eating, Ed remarked to me that I might want to try the pumpkin pie.

Not wanting to disappoint him, I agreed. Before the pie arrived, Ed warned me that it would be the best pumpkin pie I would ever eat. A bold statement, to be sure. I mean, I trusted his judgment, but the best ever? Well, I found out how correct that statement was after I took the first bite. I realized immediately this was no ordinary pumpkin pie.

I gently put the fork down while attempting to maintain my composure. Ed looked over at me with a satisfied look and asked, *"Well, what do you think?"* I had to admit that it was indeed the best pumpkin pie I had ever tasted, and I only needed one bite to realize it. Now, I believe that most people, given the proper ingredients, could probably make a decent pumpkin pie. I'm just not sure everyone could make a life-changing one. Or at least one that could make me contemplate the meaning of mastery and craft and how some of us function at levels of greatness that few ever reach. Whoever made the pumpkin pie that day was no ordinary baker. They created something remarkable and so delicious that I couldn't stop thinking about it for months afterward. It made me think about what separates the ordinary from the extraordinary.

What are the essential ingredients of success? I found a compelling answer in poet Reyna Biddy, who said this: *"Trust in your craft enough to admire it, study it, perfect it, breathe it. Never stop getting better at whatever it is that you love to do."* I don't think it matters if you're flipping burgers, writing screenplays, conducting orchestras, teaching high school science, roasting coffee, or painting houses. We all should be following Biddy's advice. Far too many of us are content with the status quo, and I find that unfortunate.

Mastery does not reside anywhere near mediocrity. Yes, you can earn a good living being average. But why would you want to? Seriously. Nobody should ever be content with average. While I can appreciate that not everyone is prepared to do whatever it takes to master their craft, I believe that mastery is attainable for those who work hard at it.

There is a myriad of factors that are involved in an individual's journey to mastery, but there is one essential that is the fuel you'll need to get you to the

Promised Land. Passion. Without it, you won't be able to sustain the energy and drive required for the road ahead. The ability to find your passion is really about finding your authentic self. You will also have to add in some resolve, a heaping amount of determination, and equal parts optimism, then top it off with some love and bake it for thirty years. Harris knows how mastery plays a role in both education and marketing and shared this *"As educators, we should never stop learning. In fact, the power of knowledge will continue to be a key ingredient for success. Students need to remember that learning doesn't end when you receive a diploma. Whether you're marketing experiences, apparel, or even food, the best companies understand that consumers seek value and quality. When you have quality products that are unique in some way compared to the competition, it makes our job as marketers easier to craft a memorable story that connects with an audience."* I will always be grateful to those who consistently show up every day willing to put the time in, who are always looking for ways to improve their skills, and who are profoundly invested in the outcome of the service they provide or product they make.

Those who take the status quo and turn it into status whoa. They never settle for good enough, and they are always looking for ways to improve both themselves and the people they work around.

If it weren't for them, the world would be a pretty sad place. In that world, I would never have had the opportunity to experience how truly incredible a slice of pumpkin pie could taste when it's baked with mastery.

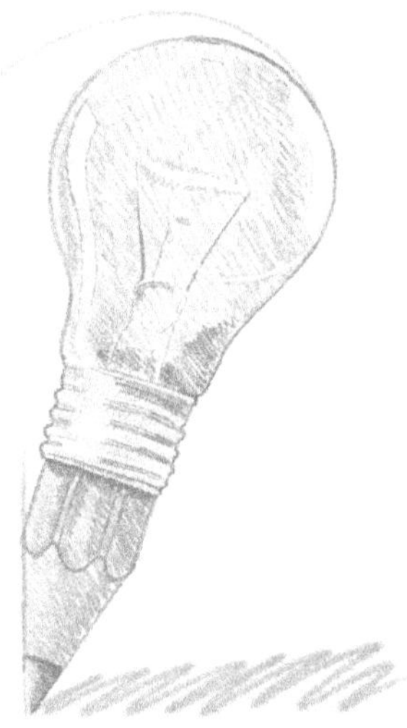

L E S S O N S
LEARNED

The ability to teach others,
while remaining teachable
yourself is critical in
nurturing continuous growth.

4

BRAINSTORMING DOES NOT WORK FOR IDEA GENERATING

In 1939, Alex Osborn, an advertising executive, had grown frustrated by the inability of individuals in his advertising agency to come up with good ideas. In response, he created the concept of a group creativity technique he called "brainstorming." In traditional brainstorming, all the participants in the group must feel comfortable openly sharing their thoughts, or it doesn't work. You can't shove people into a room and expect them to spontaneously pop out great ideas, which is why it's time to look at better approaches to idea generation.

Gary Duke, partner and chief talent officer at Wild Blue Yonder, who leads training programs and teaches creative thinking and communication skills, agrees. *"I'd argue that brainstorming never really worked all that well, but it took advancements in neuroscience to make us realize the methodology is flawed."* For example, to tap into our greatest creative potential, the right lobe of our brain needs to be fully engaged. Yet, in traditional brainstorming, people take turns speaking up and throwing ideas out. Since our verbal capabilities are housed in the left side of the brain, when we speak, we override the right lobe, and the resulting ideas we conceive are compromised. A new approach that's getting attention is called BrainSwarming®, developed by Dr. Anthony McCaffrey, an innovation researcher and professor at UMass Amherst in Massachusetts. In BrainSwarming®, a goal is posted or written down and disseminated, and people are encouraged to contribute an idea so others can see it and add to it. The technique works well for introverts and leverages the best aspects of human innovation skills.

Studies have shown that BrainSwarming® can produce up to 115 ideas in fifteen minutes versus brainstorming, which, on average, produces one hundred ideas in sixty minutes. Gary is also seeing a shift in how corporations view creativity and innovation. *"I think the greatest motivation behind this shift is fear, which is always an effective motivator. Companies realize that if they don't nurture creativity in every area of the organization, they'll be left behind."* Mind-Mapping is another technique used in a group setting or by an individual. With Mind-Mapping, a central word or phrase gets written down, and the task is to explore connections related to the goal. It's a type of free-form thinking that is highly effective in generating solid ideas.

Nichole Smith, former marketing manager at Sustainable Energy Fund, is a big fan of Mind-Mapping. *"I generally use mind maps to get a flow going when I need ideas for either copy or design imagery. They help me organize my thoughts visually. Honestly, mind-mapping is fun for me. When I am just stuck on one idea or one perspective, I get a mind-map started, and one word leads to another, then that word branches off to ten more words, then connections are made, and suddenly a brilliant idea is born*," said Smith. Brainswarming® and Mind-Mapping are practical tools in the hunt for new ideas because they give people a chance to think and work at their own pace. As the shift away from traditional brainstorming accelerates, these two techniques will undoubtedly lead to more constructive ideas by tapping into a more natural way our brains like to work.

L E S S O N S
LEARNED

Sometimes, you can draw more
inspiration from the people
who don't believe in you, then
from the ones who do.

5

COMEDY IS NO LAUGHING MATTER

It takes a unique individual to stand on a darkened stage, trying to make complete strangers laugh. It's the ultimate high-wire act performed without the benefit of a net. You must be equal parts creative, vulnerable, fearless, and intuitive.

Which is why I reached out to stand-up comedian Liz Russo, an Easton, PA, native who regularly headlines comedy clubs across the country, to learn more about the serious side of comedy. Liz believes that perseverance, intuition, and fearlessness are the essential traits required for comedians. *"Doing comedy as a full-time profession means sacrificing normality and stability. Friends and family won't understand your lifestyle. You won't be able to explain the industry or the process, and it can feel like a struggle every day."*

She also mentions how good comedians excel at turning rejection into opportunity. *"The first time I ever did stand-up comedy was a response to a heckler. During a college improv show, an audience member yelled out that I was 'the fat girl from Wilson Phillips. I felt humiliated. When I recovered from my self-pity,*

I wanted to use that feeling for something good. I wrote my first stand-up material, and the performance earned respect from the heckler as well as my peers. I found I could use humor to challenge stereotypes and social viewpoints. That is the moment where my passion met my purpose." Comedians play a far greater role in the psychological health of society than most people realize. They are experts at restructuring and reframing sad or tragic situations into humorous observations and stories.

Comedians often accomplish on stage what can often require years of therapy. Liz agrees. *"Humor is the most powerful tool in communication because it breaks down social barriers and stigma."* Comedians possess an innate ability to take simple, everyday situations and turn them into cathartic experiences that have the power to change perceptions and alter stereotypes. Laughter's medicinal benefits are significant and very real as well.

More than just a temporary break from sadness and pain, laughter provides you with the courage and strength that can go a long way to help you find new meaning and hope in your life. While every comedian's goal is to entertain you with laughter, there can be a dark side.

"It's tough when a room full of people turn against you," she says. *"As a professional, if you're paid for a contractual forty-five minutes of stage time, you must find a way through it. The worst shows earned me experience you can't get in a classroom or learn from a book. Most importantly, as hard as it was, I kept going. I never thought of quitting."* In comedy, there's always going to be a certain amount of risk-taking required and a significant amount of vulnerability coupled with a healthy dose of self-deprecation. Liz is acutely aware of what's required of her every time she steps onto a stage. *"I love making people laugh;*

I love that what I say can influence an audience to think differently and bring people together," she says. "However, if the expectation is for me to be funny and entertaining off-stage when I'm socializing, many would be disappointed that I prefer to be in my jammies watching a documentary with my cats."

L E S S O N S
LEARNED

Advertising is the one industry where all the experts seem to be the people who don't work in it.

6

THE POWER OF IMAGINATION

Back in 2012, there was a nine-year-old boy named Caine Monroy who constructed an entire arcade out of cardboard in front of his father's used auto parts store in East Los Angeles. One day, as Caine was sitting out front waiting for anyone to play his arcade, Nirvan Mullick, a local filmmaker, wandered into the store to buy a door handle for his 1996 Corolla. Caine's father was often so busy working to keep his auto parts business going that he never fully realized what Caine was doing with all that cardboard that he was fishing out of the dumpster in the back of the store.

Mullick became Caine's first customer. Because most of the auto parts business gets done online, Caine didn't get much foot traffic to his arcade. Mullick was so impressed with Caine's creativity and ingenuity that he decided that he was going to put Caine's story on video. Neither of them could realize at the time how their lives were going to change once that ten-minute video got uploaded to the internet.

People were overwhelmed by Caine's imagination. Mullick also decided he was going to help Caine realize his dream by helping him get customers to come out to play. He organized a flash mob to show up at the arcade in the hopes of giving Caine the surprise of his life. Caine's reaction on the video as he pulls up to his arcade and sees the hundreds of children and adults waiting in line for him to open the arcade is pure cinema magic. It's hard not to get emotional watching it. If you've never seen the video, you can view it at Caine's Arcade. The video quickly went viral and was viewed over a million times in twenty-four hours. In the span of two days, Caine took his imagination and love of arcades, and a global movement was born. Caine and Mullick have since traversed the globe, giving speeches at numerous colleges and universities and business summits; they even did a TED Teen Talk.

Shortly after the video's release, $240,000 was donated to Caine's college scholarship fund after people saw his imagination and wanted to help this young man pay for a college education. Caine's story is the ultimate example of thinking outside the box. I don't think there's any doubt that Caine is going to do great things with his life. He's accomplished so much already, and he just got started. Caine is now fourteen years old, spends his time in middle school, and looks forward every year to the Global Cardboard Challenge that engages over 500,000 kids in seventy countries to dream big and create something from their imaginations entirely out of cardboard.

Shortly after the video was posted in 2012, Nirvan Mullick observed, *"Any moment can be transformed into an opportunity to change the life of a child or to come up with the next big idea. Sometimes, all it takes is a little imagination."*

7

UNLOCK YOUR CREATIVITY

1. Ruts. They are easy to get into and tough to get out of. A rut will sap your energy and your vigor. Ruts are a destructive force when it comes to your creativity. It starts with keeping negative thoughts in check. They have the power to envelop you and take you down the rabbit hole of darkness. Be proactive. Take different routes to work, take brisk walks at lunch, do anything to help keep negative thoughts from taking over your well-being. Steer clear of other negative people who may have ulterior motives.

2. Ego. This one can do a lot of damage. I've witnessed too much ego take over and overshadow someone's talent. It can wreak havoc on a creative team or department. It's also been my experience that the most talented people usually have the tiniest egos. Seems the more confident you are in your skills, the less need there is for you to brag about them.

3. Fear of failure. The very nature of creativity requires that you be willing to embrace failure. Nobody loves to fail, but it is necessary if you hope to succeed. I can tell you that I still struggle with rejection. I've just learned to get over it faster when it happens, but don't think for a second that I enjoy it. Electric car inventor and space engineer Elon Musk, founder of Tesla Motors and SpaceX, said this: *"If something is important enough, you should still try, even if the probable outcome is failure."*

4. Lack of courage. Businesses today are in need of people who have the courage to stand up and champion their ideas. If you're not capable of presenting your concepts with passion, how can you expect someone else to get excited about them? Courage will help you get past the fear of the unknown by pushing you to go beyond the conventional. Your courage is one of the things that will help you stand out. No new idea stands a chance of becoming reality if the person who thought of it isn't willing to stand up and fight for it.

5. Rules. Sometimes, rules get in the way of innovation. There's a big difference, however, between rules and laws. I want to be clear about that one. History is filled with examples of people who broke the rules and changed the world for the better. Too many to cover in this space. The Dalai Lama was once quoted as telling someone, "You should learn all the rules so you know how to break them properly." The most challenging part you will face when trying to bring creativity into the workplace is the knowledge that not everyone is going to share your enthusiasm about it. Don't let that slow you down. The world needs people with the courage to stare down their fears and move forward. The road to innovation will always be under construction. Stay positive, stay humble, and never settle is the best advice I can offer.

8

DO WORK THAT FEEDS YOUR SOUL, NOT YOUR EGO

Of all the bad traits that have the potential to damage your career or prevent you from earning respect from your peers, a giant ego could be the worst. Just to be clear, I'm not talking about confidence here; I'm talking about an exaggerated sense of self-importance. Confidence is healthy; an out-of-control ego is not.

Confidence says, "I'm valuable" while ego says, "I'm invaluable." Big difference. Doing creative work involves a certain amount of risk, and having an inflated ego can be extremely limiting to that process. If you're unwilling to allow yourself to be viewed as vulnerable, it can often limit you if you hope to do serious, groundbreaking, and fulfilling work.

Dr. Brené Brown, a research professor at the University of Houston who has spent the last thirteen years studying vulnerability, said this: *"Vulnerability is not weakness. That myth is profoundly dangerous. Vulnerability is the birthplace of innovation, creativity, and change."*

LESSONS LEARNED

Curiosity is the catalyst that
will get you to see things in
a new perspective.

Just as failure and success are linked, so are vulnerability and strength. People with amplified egos are not comfortable asking for help or admitting they don't possess skills. Their egos take over, and they tend to judge everyone and everything based on appearance, possessions, and other superficial aspects.

There's an excellent scene in the movie Indiana Jones and the Last Crusade when Harrison Ford, playing Indiana Jones, must choose the right Grail to save his dying father, played by Sean Connery. The villain picks first and chooses a cup adorned with rubies and emeralds, beautifully shaped and what he thought represented the cup of a king. He chose poorly, as the knight standing guard remarks to Indy after he gets reduced to ash right in front of them. Harrison Ford then looks for the cup of a carpenter. He selects an old, misshapen, dirty cup, and it turns out to be the one that saves his father's life. He chose correctly. I think people can be like those cups. Don't be the one that represents ego, pride, greed, or narcissism. Be the one that represents humility, gratitude, and vulnerability. It makes a huge difference in how you approach your work.

My strategy has always been to work with those who are better than me. I'm at peace with the fact that I will never know everything, but I'm smart enough to know that strength comes from humility and gratitude towards my coworkers and the work we produce together. I've had the pleasure, over the years, to work with some of the most talented artists, designers, copywriters, editors, photographers, actors, and directors the Lehigh Valley (PA) has ever produced, and I learned something from every single one of them. In fact, I'm still learning and will do so until the day I die.

Here's how I work on keeping my ego in check. I have an attitude of gratitude, I don't feel like I always need to be right, I surrender my need for control, I work on being a better me and less on trying to be better than everyone else around me, and I always try to be open to constructive criticism. These are simple things, but they can have an impact. Besides, the best type of work is the kind that feeds your soul, not your ego.

9

GIVE CREATIVITY THE RESPECT IT DESERVES

Imagine a power so strong that no army can defeat it. Imagine that this power never gets depleted. In fact, the more you use it, the more you have of it. Who wouldn't want that type of unlimited power? Well, that same power happens to reside inside all of us. I'm speaking, of course, about creativity. The first use of the word "creativity" was by the seventeenth-century poet Maciej Sarbiewski — but he applied it only to describe the creation of poetry. For over a century and a half, people rejected the idea of human creativity because the term "creation" was reserved for creating "from nothing."

Human creativity has been studied and explored in countless books, podcasts, websites, and magazines in both the public and the private sectors. We've crossed the event horizon, and creativity is now an accepted way to drive change and innovation. The fields of music, science, technology, architecture, art, business, education, literature, medicine, and engineering are necessary for our country's continued growth and prosperity.

L E S S O N S
LEARNED

People will tell you something is impossible do so because they are too afraid to try it themselves.

People like Steve Jobs, Louis Pasteur, Nikola Tesla, George Washington Carver, Marie Curie, Frank Lloyd Wright, Miles Davis, Ayn Rand, Alan Turing, Amelia Earhart, Maya Angelou, Pablo Picasso, etc. They all used significant amounts of creativity to break through the limitations they encountered to make invaluable contributions that enhanced our world. None of them escaped ridicule.

It doesn't matter if you're a Nobel Prize-winning physicist working on the Higgs boson particle or a middle-school student working on your next science fair project. Both must tap into their creative capacity if they hope to stand out from the herd. Today, the demand for people who are willing to lead us beyond what we think we're capable of achieving is in high order. We need those people who won't accept the "well, we've always done it that way" mentality.

Good leaders know that sometimes they will have to bend a few rules to help us push past our limitations. None of us can change the world by being safely ensconced inside our comfort zone. Innovation is messy. It doesn't follow a straight path and certainly won't track neatly onto a spreadsheet.

We need to consider that our world has seen more change in the last one hundred years than in the previous billion years, and creativity is leading the charge. In the groundbreaking book titled The Rise of the Creative Class, author Richard Florida, considered one of the world's leading experts on economic competitiveness and technological innovation, explored the rise of creativity as a fundamental economic force and discovered that creativity is indeed experiencing a renaissance.

"Human creativity is the most spectacularly transformative force ever unleashed, and it is something that all of us can draw on to one degree or another. So if the rise of this new order and new social class poses tremendous challenges, it carries the seeds of its resolution as well," said Florida.

Thankfully, even though creativity is now being taken seriously as an economic driver, more work needs to be done before creativity receives the full status it deserves. Unfortunately, the old stereotype of creative people sitting around on their beanbag chairs looking for meaning through the incandescent glow of their lava lamps still lingers. Creativity can be intimidating to people who don't fully understand it. Ask Greek philosopher and mathematician Pythagoras how it went for him when he proposed the radical idea that the Earth was not flat in 500 B.C.

Every revolution has its critics. This one is no different. Accessing your creative resources is one of the best options anyone can use to separate themselves from the dross of mediocrity that often permeates society. I'm excited to see more examples where creativity gets the proper status it rightly deserves.

The most challenging part anyone will ever face when trying to bring creativity into a workplace is the knowledge that not everyone will share your enthusiasm about it. Don't let that stop you.

The world needs people with the guts to stare down their fear of failure and move forward anyway. Stay positive, stay humble, and never settle. Remember, we're hardwired to avoid failure because of the criticism that usually follows it. So don't be fooled; it's the critics who carry all the fear.

10

CREATIVITY THRIVES WHEN YOU STEP OUTSIDE YOUR COMFORT ZONE

When was the last time you tried something for the first time? When was the last time you tried something new without knowing what the outcome was going to be? Too often, we tend to do what is safe, what is known. I'm pretty sure that our willingness to stay within our comfort zones has its origins in prehistoric times. Back then, staying safe inside your cave made sense when venturing out meant you could end up as a T-Rex's lunch. Fast forward a couple of millennia, and I think many of us are still playing it too safe. Now, what might be a good idea for your average Neanderthal doesn't work today. In the heating and air-conditioning industry, there's a term used to describe the perfect temperature.

It's when the temperature is such that no heating or cooling is necessary for the home. It's aptly named the "comfort zone." Do you know what happens in the comfort zone? Absolutely nothing. Humans also have comfort zones, and they can be detrimental to

LESSONS
LEARNED

Mediocre ideas lack the emotional voltage needed to motivate us to take action.

us by holding us back from experiencing new things that challenge us. So what can you do about it? The good news is that comfort zones are expandable. Once your comfort zone expands, it won't shrink back to its original size.

Creativity is the perfect tool to help you expand your comfort zone. Being creative is about being open to new adventures or exciting challenges. The more time you spend outside your comfort zone will be the best way for you to open yourself up to greater fulfillment and improved well-being.

Being able to go consistently outside your comfort zone is a skill that can be applied to most careers because so few people are willing to do it. The technique itself requires courage, self-reflection, and a level of persistence that makes most people uncomfortable. Author John Gardner said this in his book Self-Renewal regarding risk avoidance: *"It is a powerful obstacle to growth. It assures the progressive narrowing of the personality and prevents exploration and experimentation."*

So here's what I want you to try. Starting today, I want you to think of something that you can do that would expand your comfort zone. Doesn't have to be anything crazy. The key is to add something into your life that will challenge you in a real way. Try a different type of food. Check out a genre of film you wouldn't normally watch. Listen to a different style of music or reconnect with an old friend or college roommate that you haven't talked to in a while. Keep in mind that the whole point of the exercise is that you are doing something that makes you uncomfortable.

Choosing to live outside your comfort zone requires effort. It won't always be easy, and there will be setbacks. Escape the restrictive patterns that can hold you back and seize the opportunities that lie hidden in the obstacles. Start small and work your way up. Once you start to do it with enough consistency, it will become second nature, and you'll be on your way to living a more creative life.

11

THE 4 PILLARS OF CREATIVITY

Even if you feel like creativity isn't necessary in your life, lots of people are finding ways to use it to solve problems and challenges in today's modern workplace. We all possess the potential to tap our creative power, and there's no better way to create those opportunities than to start viewing life through the lens of creativity. Here are four traits that I think are vital as you explore your creative potential.

Wonderment. There is nothing more essential to creativity than wonderment. It's the ability to reconnect with the past, to remember what it felt like when the world was new to you. If you can reach back into your childhood, then you can touch genius. As adults, we forget the power of wonderment and how it connects us to the magic that surrounds us every day. Albert Einstein summed it up perfectly: *"The most beautiful thing we can experience is the mysterious. It is the source of all true art and science. He to whom the emotion is a stranger, who can no longer pause to wonder and stand wrapped in awe, is as good as dead."*

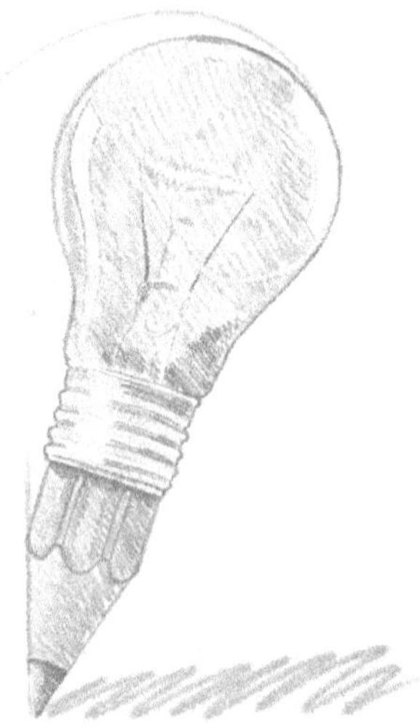

L E S S O N S
LEARNED

**Creativity is about input,
not output.**

Courage. This trait will help you stay on the trail as you hunt down your big ideas. It's an important quality because new ideas are so fragile. They are easy to kill by a sneer or condescending word. Courage will help you take the necessary risks and provide you with the strength you will need to persevere when others would have you quit. Courage is the fuel you'll use to start something new, even when you're not sure you will succeed.

Authenticity. Creativity demands authenticity. As you work on developing ideas or finding new ways to solve problems, you must be authentic in how you approach those challenges. Authentic people are not afraid to speak their minds, which is critical as you look to build trust with your team. Genuine people will tell you what you need to hear, not what you want to hear. Dr. Brené Brown offers this cautionary thought: *"If you trade your authenticity for safety, you may experience the following: anxiety, depression, eating disorders, rage, blame, resentment and inexplicable grief."*

Curiosity. A trait that's essential if you hope to be more creative. Also a quality that harkens back to childhood when our curiosity was at its peak. Leo Burnett, a Chicago ad agency executive and founder of the firm that still bears his name, said this: *"Curiosity about life in all of its aspects, I think, is still the secret of all great creative people."* It's as simple as ABC: Always. Be. Curious. Just as a fire needs oxygen to burn, creativity needs curiosity, and creativity won't work unless you do.

The traits I've discussed above can help anyone looking to become more creative. When I was growing up, it felt like creativity was used mostly for creating artwork. Today, it gets used for so much more as our society is finally embracing it and using it in unconventional ways. As the world continues to accelerate and evolve, creativity will lead the way. Have the courage to take the journey. Be fearlessly authentic, and let your wonderment and curiosity be your guide.

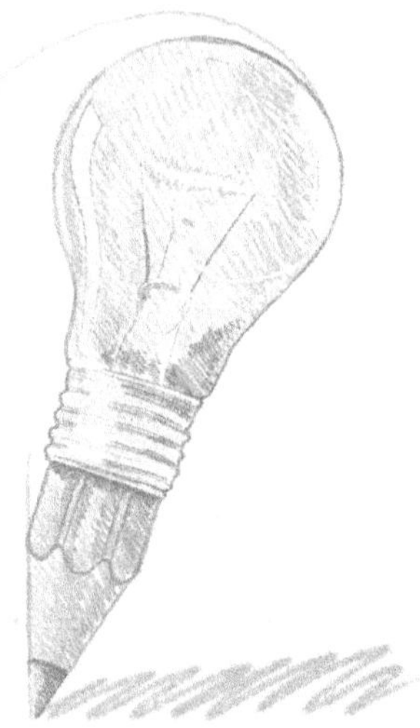

L E S S O N S
LEARNED

Great advertising is always it's own call to action.

12

EMBRACE THE CONSTRAINTS

In Greek mythology, the nine Muses were Greek goddesses who ruled over the arts and sciences and offered inspiration in those subjects. Calliope is the Muse who presides over eloquence and epic poetry. She's considered the "Chief of all Muses." I know because she's visited me from time to time. Anyone looking to engage in a creative capacity needs inspiration. But inspiration can be extremely elusive. I will freely admit to you that there are some days when it feels like I've entirely run out of ideas. It's just the natural ebb and flow of the creative process. Early in my career, that used to bother me. I thought that I had run out of ideas. Now, I know better. Contrary to conventional thinking, constraints are the key to big ideas. But what creates the conditions that allow inspiration to appear? Can it be summoned up at will?

I believe you can set the conditions for inspiration by working within constraints. I know that nobody likes to work with restrictions, but the truth is they can be extremely beneficial. When limitations are present, you dedicate your mental energy to acting more resourcefully. Obstacles broaden perception and open your mind to look at challenges with a renewed focus.

L E S S O N S
LEARNED

Advertising that does not make you think, will not compel you to act.

A lack of options is the grit that grinds the wheel of inspiration. When your options are limited, you're compelled to use creativity to deliver a solution that fits the parameters. Sometimes, an idea can come quickly; other times, a sustained effort is what's required. The quality of your thoughts will always be in direct proportion to the amount of energy you are willing to invest in discovering them.

Mediocre ideas are usually the first to show up, followed closely by acceptable ideas. Don't stop at acceptable. Push for the more exceptional idea. Just know that it won't be easy. You'd be surprised how many times I improved on an idea that I had already considered solved. The worst thing you can do is to try and force an idea into existence. I've tried, and it doesn't work. There are only so many hours you can spend staring at a blank piece of paper or the cursor on your computer screen, waiting for inspiration to show up, that sometimes it's best to sleep on it and start fresh the next day. Plus, I think a Muse will only descend when she knows you're struggling and earnestly in search of something big.

When you feel exhausted and still have nothing to show for your effort, that's when getting some outside opinions might be helpful. In most cases, their thoughts may spark something new, and that could take you down a path you hadn't considered. Don't let frustration creep in and taint the process. Stay the course.

I have always believed that ideas can come from anyone. Be open to outside opinions. Seek feedback, even if it's negative. Bill Bernbach, creative director of Doyle Dane Bernbach (DDB), used to carry a slip a paper in his shirt pocket that said, *"They might be right."* It was a way to remind himself to be open to different opinions. Ray Dalio, the founder of investment firm Bridgewater Associates, one of the world's largest hedge funds, offers this: *"More than anything else, what differentiates people who live up to their potential from those who don't is a willingness to look at themselves and others objectively."*

Objectivity and constraints are huge elements that go into producing the best ideas. Idea generating is often your willingness to be ready to go when the mood or Muse strikes. That may not always fit neatly into a nine-to-five workday. A constricted timeline or lack of resources will always force creativity to show up sooner. You must still be willing to put considerable effort into solving the challenge if you hope to discover a transformational idea; at least, that's what my Muse told me.

13

CREATIVITY IS THE REAL STAR IN GROUNDHOG DAY

In 1993, Groundhog Day, a movie starring Bill Murray, was released in theaters nationwide. It was an immediate hit. Countless numbers of people have developed theories over the years about the underlying metaphors present in the film. Spiritual, psychological, and even religious overtones have been discussed in blogs and podcasts. I can appreciate those comparisons, but I have a different theory. I think the movie illustrates how someone can use creativity to alter undesirable situations. I'm not sure if that's what Harold Ramis intended, but that's the connection I've made. If you've never seen the film, it's worth viewing.

**(Spoiler alert: major plot points
are about to be revealed.)**

In it, Bill Murray plays a cranky weatherman named Phil Conners from Pittsburgh who gets sent to Punxsutawney, Pennsylvania, to cover the Groundhog Day activities. As he and his production crew try to leave for home, they are forced to turn back due to a blizzard

59

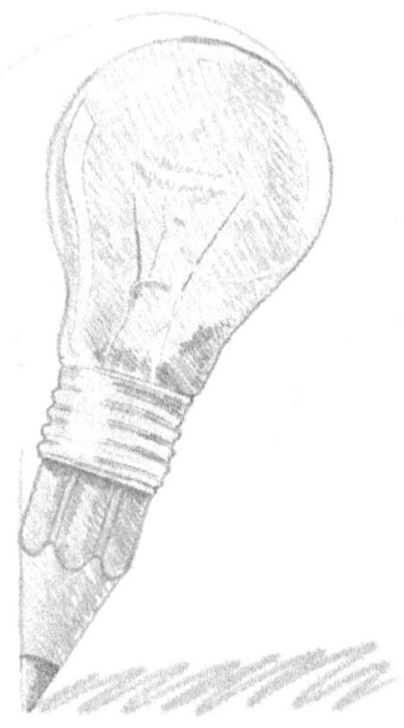

L E S S O N S
LEARNED

Nothing you do will ever be appreciated by someone who never valued you in the first place.

that closes the interstate. Murray's character is then forced to spend the rest of the day interacting with the people in Punxsutawney. When he wakes up the next morning, the day resets back to where it started. When I first saw the movie, I thought it was a genius concept. Bill Murray tries everything he can think of to not have to keep reliving that same day over and over. At one point, he even runs his car off a steep cliff, only to wake up the next morning to begin the whole process again. When I viewed the movie through the lens of creativity, my theory took shape. The film spends a tremendous amount of time showing Murray as he tries to come to grips with his dilemma. Each and every time, he's met with failure as he winds up in his bed the next morning with the clock reset to the previous day at 6:00 a.m. Near the end of the film, after he has exhausted what he believes is every possible option he can think of to alter his situation, a change of heart occurs.

He ends his cycle of suffering and starts cooperating with the present. That's the key he uses to turn everything around. By engaging his creativity, a whole new world opens up to Murray, and he's transformed from the curmudgeonly newscaster into the best version of himself he can be. Nothing about his surroundings or the people in the town has changed. The one thing that did change was his attitude toward having to live the same day over and over. It's an intense exercise in self-reflection. Creativity drove the change he needed to turn it all around. What a perfect way to illustrate what can happen when you refuse to accept a bad situation by using a little imagination to live up to your full potential.

How many of us are living the same day over and over and never experiencing the type of change we so desperately crave? Embrace the transformative power that creativity offers by refusing to accept mediocrity in any situation, and I promise you, a new day will dawn.

L E S S O N S
LEARNED

It's not about survival of the fittest. It's about survival for those who are strong enough to ask for help when they need it.

14

TOP 5 MYTHS SURROUNDING CREATIVITY

The creative process can be mysterious and intimidating. But if you understand how it works, it can also greatly improve both your work and personal life. Here's a look at the top five myths I've encountered regarding creativity.

No. 1: Creative people always have great ideas. If only that were true. But the creative process doesn't work like that. Sure, there are some days when all my neurons are firing across my corpus callosum and I feel like I could solve the world's toughest problems. The flip side of that coin is that there are days when I feel like I have completely run out of ideas. Early in my career, those days scared me. I didn't fully comprehend why one day, I could feel so creative, only to be met with the opposite feeling a day later. I had to learn to respect the process of ebb and flow. Now, I recognize what's happening and try to use it to my advantage.

No. 2: Idea-generating is best done in a group. I know that this runs counter to conventional thinking.

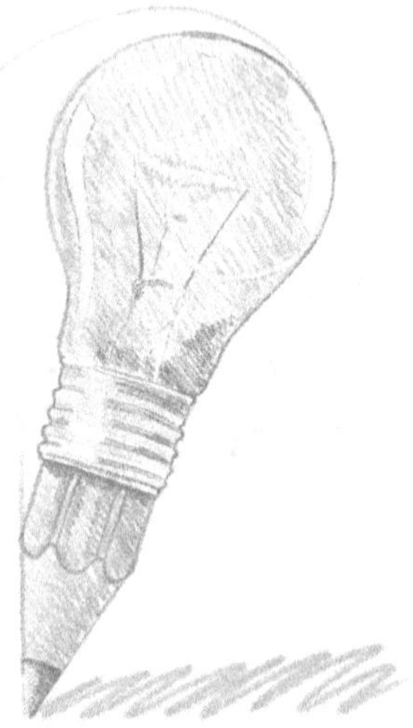

L E S S O N S
LEARNED

There is no such thing as failure. Only unintended outcomes.

I do think that a group brainstorm can work if everyone in the group trusts and respects each other, but most people aren't that comfortable sharing their thoughts openly. Sometimes, you just have to hunker down after the noise of the day has abated and allow your mind to quiet. Ideas will not easily flow out of a cluttered mind.

No. 3: Drugs can help you be more creative. Nope. What drugs will do, however, is make you feel like you're being more creative when, in fact, you're not. Drugs will lower your inhibitions, which most people mistake for the feeling of being creative and free. When you're intoxicated, your thinking becomes less clear. You will not do your best thought-generation under the influence of drugs or alcohol – it's that simple.

No. 4: Creativity is only for artists. John G. Young, the former CEO of Hewlett-Packard, said, "The development of creative problem-solving skills is now a necessity, not a luxury." We all have two distinct hemispheres of our brain. The right side controls thought, intuition, and creativity. The left side controls logic, rationality and objectivity. Most careers today require both.

No. 5: Creativity can't be developed. This one's a doozy. Think about it – anything you put time into learning can be developed. It all comes down to how hard you're willing to work at it. People who find themselves living mostly out of the right side of their brain can tap into their creativity fairly easily, while those living primarily out of the left side might have to work a little more. But, just like other skills, creativity can be learned.

I'm not sure why there are so many myths surrounding creativity or how it got to be so misunderstood, but don't be afraid to spend some time working on your creative side. You have to be willing to push yourself out of your comfort zone — that's the best way to break out of old, established patterns.

L E S S O N S
LEARNED

In school, the test comes after the lesson. In life, the lesson comes after the test.

15

CREATIVITY CAN DRIVE EDUCATION REFORM

It always hurts my soul when I hear that a school decides to cut back on creative classes like music and art. After all, allowing kids to be creative in school helps set them up to become creative adults. The current public educational system in the United States was developed in the nineteenth century primarily to meet the demands of the Industrial Revolution. The spread of industry necessitated mass schooling to produce a skilled workforce. The system worked: factories had workers and workers had permanent jobs.

Today, the global economy demands new ideas and innovation, but our educational system doesn't encourage entrepreneurial traits like creativity, risk-taking, or leadership. The system is more concerned with teaching kids how to take standardized tests than helping them nurture their passions. I don't blame the teachers; I blame those who refuse to admit that the world has changed and that we should keep doing the same thing over and over and expect different results.

L E S S O N S
LEARNED

Metrics are a window to the past; ideas are a doorway to the future.

Irish poet William Butler Yeats got it right: "Education is not the filling of a pail, but the lighting of a fire." A wonderful example of what Mr. Yeats is referring to is in Jack Foster's fantastic book titled How to Get Ideas, where he writes about an exercise he calls "What is half of 13?" The purpose of the exercise is not to find the correct answer; Foster already knows the answer is 6.5. Instead, he's more interested in seeing if we can solve it creatively.

Since schools are not required to encourage creative thought, it's hard for us to imagine how to solve the challenge. When you view it through a creative lens, the clues begin to reveal themselves. The number 1 is half of 13. The number 3 is half of 13. What about thir or how about teen? What if you wrote the number thirteen and erased the bottom half? What about Roman numerals? Thirteen is written like this: XIII, so "X" is half of thirteen and "III" is half of thirteen. The exercise is designed to show that when you look to solve a challenge creatively, you must be willing to look at it from different angles and be open to new possibilities, which is precisely what young children do effortlessly.

Think back on your childhood and how you could play for hours with an empty refrigerator box. You could use it to create a boat, a car, a rocket ship, a castle. Endless possibilities. That's the beauty of imagination and creativity, which is why, if you can reach back into your childhood, you can taste genius. Children's book author and creativity expert Vince Gowmon states, *"Children do not move, think, or speak in a straight line, and neither does imagination or creativity. Sadly, though, our standardized pathways of education still do."*

In one of the most-viewed TED talks ever given, "Do Schools Kill Creativity?" Sir Ken Robinson, who led an advisory committee on creative and cultural reform, said,

"Our children and teachers are encouraged to follow routine algorithms rather than to excite that power of imagination and curiosity." He added, *"Young children are wonderfully confident in their imaginations....Most of us lose this confidence as we grow up."*

The next few years in our country are going to be crucial. It's time for creativity to be granted its proper status in education. It's every bit as important as math, science, history, and social studies.

While the Industrial Revolution is over, now is an excellent time to re-engineer how we structure our curriculums. Curiosity, wonderment, and imagination should no longer be viewed as mere childs play. Those attributes must be encouraged and treated with respect at every grade level if we ever hope to change the current outdated educational system and put students on a path to success.

Section 2:
Creative Leadership

So many authors have written on this topic, yet so many bad leaders are still out there ruining companies and corporate cultures with their antiquated approach of leading through fear and intimidation. A creative leader is an inspired leader who knows how to empower and motivate their people. Transform from ordinary to extraordinary by setting up a creative culture that empowers everyone to embrace their creative side.

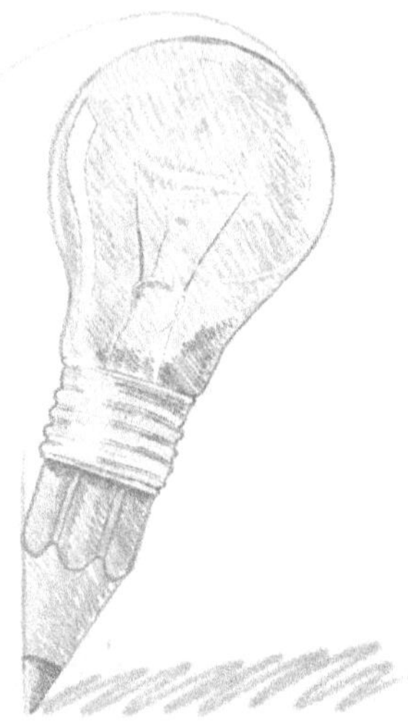

LESSONS LEARNED

The worst type of leader to work is the one who doesn't know what they don't know.

16

TOP 5 QUALITIES OF INSPIRED LEADERS

It's not enough to just have the title. Leadership is less about the position and more about the action you take that will help the people you manage achieve success. Leadership is holding people accountable to their potential and helping them to see the greatness in themselves.

Steve Borrelli, president of Borrelli Consulting, who has spent years mentoring and coaching leaders, agrees. "While I think there is much that can be learned and taught with respect to leadership, I believe some natural instinct and aptitude are key components of every great leader's personality profile. Many of the people who I've worked with and consider top-notch leaders all had a genuine passion for seeing other people succeed."

Here are the top five qualities I believe you'll need to be an effective, inspiring leader in today's workplace.

Authenticity. According to Borrelli, "By far the number one trait most critical to great leadership is AUTHENTICITY. Being genuine and authentic allows a leader to more effectively utilize all the other facets of

L E S S O N S
LEARNED

The world needs people who say it can't be done, otherwise we wouldn't strive to accomplish anything.

his or her leadership style." Without authenticity, you will struggle to earn the trust of the people you are charged with leading. Your words and your actions have meaning. Make sure what you are saying and what you are doing are in sync. If you make a mistake, own up to it. That's how respect is earned.

Passion. Passion is highly contagious. Passion gives you the courage to be fearlessly authentic. Passionate people want to work with other passionate people. That's how companies go from good to great. In almost every instance, your passion should be your profession.

Emotional Stability. Great leaders must be able to tolerate stress and frustration. Today's business climate is too volatile and wildly unpredictable. You need someone who can project confidence during challenging times. You will not inspire trust in your team if you openly complain about company issues.

Communication. In his book Why Leaders Eat Last, Simon Sinek offers, "*Communication is not about speaking what we think. Communication is about ensuring others hear what we mean.*" To which Borrelli adds, "*One of the biggest challenges for today's leaders is understanding what motivates the different generations. It seems much more pronounced than when I started in business in the early '80s. Millennials, Gen X, Gen Y, and now Gen Z all seem to have dramatically different profiles of what they care about and need in the workplace. This is a huge challenge to uncover how to get the most out of a very diverse work group.*"

Creativity. All inspired leaders know that creativity will not grow in a toxic environment. In fact, a healthy culture will always help your company retain people and attract new talent. Creativity doesn't always involve new ideas. Sometimes, it means supporting an atmosphere where people have permission to take calculated risks and even fail gloriously.

All these traits bring unique aspects to leadership and help complete the overall mission. In the end, leaders who put their people first often have people who put the customer first, and in that world, everyone wins.

17

CREATING A CULTURE OF CALCULATED RISK

There is a multitude of essential factors that need consideration when bringing a culture of creativity into your workplace. If you don't have all the elements, the initiative can struggle to bear fruit. One of those elements is a leader who can inspire his staff to be comfortable with risk. Do you openly encourage employees to share their ideas? Do employees feel comfortable telling you things you need to hear as opposed to what you want to hear? Would you ever consider rewarding an employee for a failure? Do you encourage dissenting opinions? Do you set the tone and mentor anyone who might be struggling to keep pace with their coworkers? If you said "yes" to all those questions, then you are what I would call an inspired leader.

Pat Lincoln, general manager of Connoisseur Media, is that type of leader. Lincoln manages two radio stations and a sales staff of five. He's someone who is not afraid to take risks when it comes to driving sales and creating a culture where everyone has the same opportunity to succeed.

Never take criticism from someone you wouldn't go to for advice.

"If you want a creative culture, management needs to be very secure with things like failure and listening to different ideas from people. Most organizations are not comfortable with it; they might say they are, but in reality, it proves to be quite the opposite," Lincoln says.

Lincoln told me about the time he did something with his staff that most sales managers would view as being outright reckless: *"I took away their sales quotas and goals for one year. In that time, our communication improved and new ideas flowed freely, as did our revenue, to record heights. The sales team worked harder because they didn't stop at a self-imposed limit set for them by me. They went from worrying about hitting a sales target to focusing on solving their clients' marketing challenges. In turn, clients wanted to work with them even more because our customers saw them as a valued resource instead of someone just trying to sell them radio spots."* Taking away a sales goal for a team whose primary function is to drive revenue inside an organization is risky.

The difference is that Lincoln understood the unique individuals on his team. He knew what they were capable of accomplishing, and he was more than ready to guide them if things went south. Pat also knew that for the initiative to succeed, his team had to know that they had his full support. *"I made sure that each salesperson was acutely aware that I believed in them and that they had nothing to fear. I told them to focus their energy on their clients, and the rest would take care of itself."*

Lincoln took a calculated risk and inspired his staff to believe in his decision. He didn't have a crystal ball to gaze into to predetermine what the outcome was going to be. What he did have was the belief and trust that his staff would find a way to make it work. And that made all the difference.

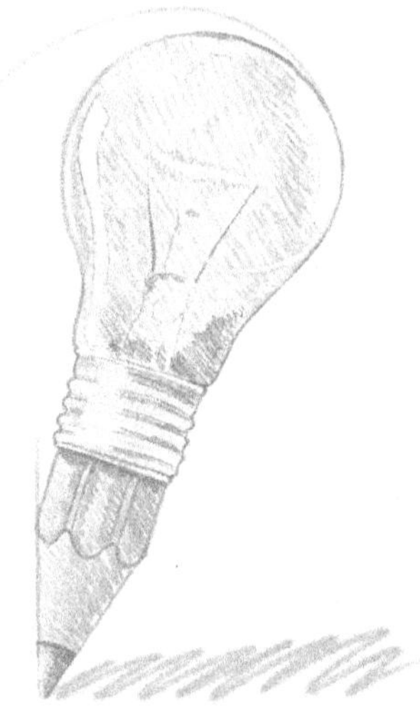

L E S S O N S
LEARNED

Weak ideas lead to typical.
Typical leads to mediocrity.
Mediocrity leads nowhere .

PLAYING THROUGH THE CHALLENGES

When Brett Bacho was eight years old, he wanted one thing. He wanted to be able to play guitar like Ace Frehley of the rock band KISS. The year was 1978, and KISS was one of the biggest bands in the world. So, after months of bugging his parents to buy him a guitar, they finally relented. *"They bought me this little red acoustic guitar from Sears that had strings that were thick and stiff like barbed wire,"* says Bacho. His parents signed him up for guitar lessons, and he was on his way.

Bacho was enjoying the lessons and progressing nicely until one day, he arrived at what he likes to call the dreaded F chord. For many reasons, the F chord is one of the toughest chords for beginners to learn how to play. *"My fingers were a little too small to play the chord properly, and I grew extremely frustrated. My instructor scolded me for not practicing enough, and I told my mom that I wanted to quit my guitar lessons,"* he adds.

What he didn't realize at that moment was that he was about to learn what can happen when you refuse to let a difficult challenge determine your next course of action.

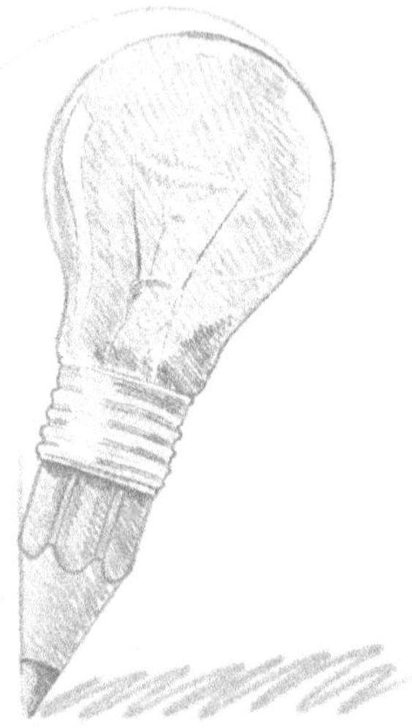

LESSONS LEARNED

Creativity is not a step in the process, it's essential to the process.

Bacho had two choices. One, he could quit, or two, he could play through the discomfort. His parents encouraged him to keep practicing, which he reluctantly did. After some trial and error, he learned to play, as he likes to say, "that F-ing chord." He got to experience a big lesson in leadership and learned at an early age how good leaders solve many of the problems they encounter every day. When frustration sets in, many of us are not in a good mental space to draw out any of the lessons that might be hidden below the surface.

These days, Bacho is the CEO and president of Kitchen Magic, a kitchen and bathroom remodeling company based in Nazareth, PA. Bacho's role does not require him to teach people how to play guitar, but he does use the lessons he learned from those years. *I have thought about that F chord whenever the team at Kitchen Magic experiences difficulty. It taught me the power of persistence, consistency, and encouragement.* There's no doubt leadership is a complicated process, and for many, it can take years to begin to understand how to generate positive, actionable results. At its core, leadership is servanthood because it's less about being in charge and more about taking care of those in your charge by setting up a culture where everyone gets treated with dignity and respect. It may sound easy, but it's not. *I am fortunate to be surrounded by great people I trust and who trust me,* observes Bacho. *I give them the encouragement and support they need and help determine their priorities. They know they can count on me to never shy away from difficult challenges.*

Leadership expert and best-selling author Simon Sinek sums leadership up like this: *"The true price of leadership is the willingness to place the needs of others above your own. Great leaders truly care about those they are privileged to lead and understand that the true cost of the leadership privilege comes at the expense of self-interest."*

The leadership Bacho provides is rooted in his deep understanding that we all experience setbacks and get frustrated when dealing with challenges at work as well as in our personal lives. His experience has taught him that the most significant lessons are learned during challenging times. Anything new you're ever going to attempt will invariably present unforeseen challenges. Stay the course. Play through the challenge.

Your success will ultimately be determined by how you choose to navigate those obstacles. Like many of life's challenges, the F chord has the power to trip us up and take us off the path. I hope that when you find yourself dealing with a frustrating situation and are unsure how to proceed, you remember that life is always ready to teach us a lesson. All you have to do is be willing and open to learn from it.

19

DISTILLING THE LESSONS OF LEADERSHIP

Chad Butters served our country proudly, flying military aircraft in the United States Army. He flew Blackhawk helicopters, among other aircraft, for a career spanning twenty-five years. It probably never crossed his mind that one day, he would own and operate a distillery. Yet, that's exactly what ended up happening.

"After I retired from active duty, I told my wife that we should put down some roots in a nice place and grow a business. I said that whatever we decide, it should involve agriculture, be family owned and operated, have some basis in science, and ultimately be fun to do," Butters says. Today, he is one of the co-owners of Eight Oaks Distillery, a farm-to-bottle craft distiller nestled in the hills of New Tripoli, PA. *"Once all those boxes got checked, we landed on the idea of starting a distillery, and to this day, I'm still amazed that my wife Jodi agreed to let me start one,"* he jokes.

While you might think that flying Blackhawk helicopters in the military has nothing to do with distilling whiskey,

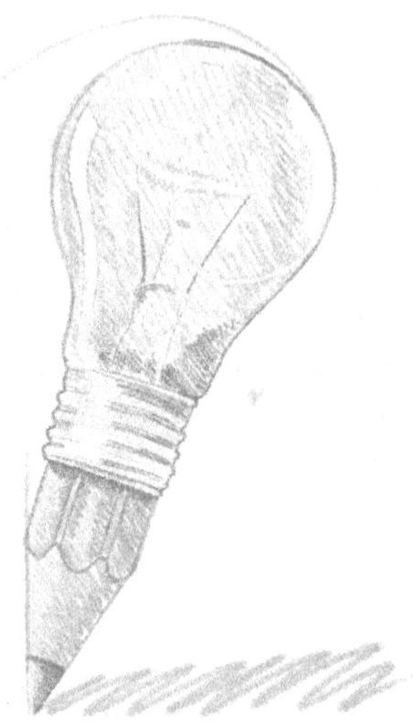

L E S S O N S
LEARNED

None of the great books written on leadership will encourage you to use fear as a prime motivator.

well, you'd be mistaken. Both require strong leadership and clearly defined missions. *"Leadership is about conveying a stable mission along with the steps for how you're going to accomplish it."* Eight Oaks' primary mission is to distill the best whiskey, gin, vodka, rum, and bourbon they possibly can.

While Butters is thrilled with how well the core business is doing, he believes in dreaming big. He and his team are playing the long game. While their primary goal is to grow the business, they also have a plan to do a B Corp certification, which is a private certification issued to for-profit companies by B Lab, a global nonprofit organization that certifies companies based on how they create value for non-shareholding stakeholders, such as their employees, the local community, and the environment. *"It's a triple-bottom-line philosophy involving financial, social, and internal initiatives,"* he says. He knows that great leadership is about serving others. He experienced it in the military, and now he distills those lessons to the employees at Eight Oaks. *"Our employees are so much more than a resource of the business. When it comes right down to it, I believe it's about authentically caring about the people you work with and knowing what's important to them and their futures."*

It's refreshing for me to hear a business owner being so candid about his leadership approach. His business philosophy is one that's hard not to respect because he's proud of what his company represents and the people who have signed on to participate in the journey.

His ultimate goal is to one day look back, many years from now, and know that people admire Eight Oaks not only for the quality of their product but also their reputation for nurturing and supporting their employees and organizations in the surrounding communities. *"True leaders are always learning,"* Butters says. *"Leaders have to be tuned into what's going on and open to using creative approaches with people based on what motivates that individual. Because I believe leadership is about cultivating meaningful relationships with your employees and customers and never assuming a 'one-size-fits-all' approach."* That's a business and leadership philosophy worthy of a toast. Make mine a double.

20

INNOVATORS DO NOT ASK FOR PERMISSION

There are people in this world whose extraordinary talent captures the world's attention. They force us to alter our perspectives through their unwillingness to accept the status quo. They are innovators and agents of change who refuse to accept mediocrity. Through their passion and their work, we can experience their genius.

Frank Lloyd Wright, without a doubt, is the world's greatest architect. Full stop. What set Frank Lloyd Wright apart from his contemporaries was that he brought American architecture to the forefront. Nature influenced his visionary designs, and he emphasized craftsmanship while making design accessible to all. During World War II, when most of the building construction slowed down, Wright began designing the Usonian houses, affordable housing that would revolutionize the American concept of domestic architecture. *"Form follows function—that has been misunderstood. Form and function should be one, joined in a spiritual union,"* Wright said. Some of his more famous projects include Taliesin, The Frederick C. Robie House, Fallingwater, The Guggenheim in

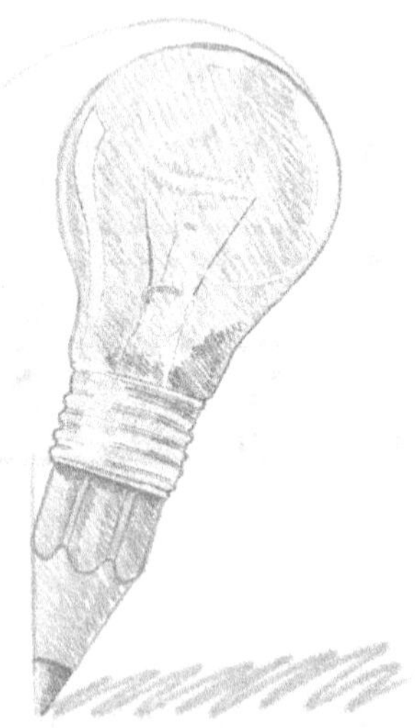

L E S S O N S
LEARNED

Creative unpredictability frightens corporate management and that's why it's so badly needed.

NYC, The Imperial Hotel in Tokyo, and Johnson Wax Headquarters. Each one is unique in its own way and groundbreaking on every level.

Lee Clow is considered to be the advertising industry's gentleman godfather and current chairman and global director of TBWA\Worldwide. He's worked on some of the most iconic brands in the last forty years, and he's still going strong. His "1984" Apple Computer TV spot is considered by industry experts to be the best ad ever created. The commercial introduced the world to the MacIntosh computer.

It was groundbreaking at the time because it never showed anyone using the actual product. Clow continues to find the business fun and challenging. He believes we are at the beginning of the most exciting time the advertising business has ever seen. While lots of people are talking about the challenge of the multimedia future, he believes it is the biggest opportunity for creative minds since the first creative revolution of the 1960s.

Dale Chihuly is considered by many to be the world's premier glass artist. Chihuly has led the development of glass as a fine art. While he has exhibited his groundbreaking work all over the world, he currently has work on display at the New York Botanical Garden in the Bronx, New York. His unique approaches to techniques in glassblowing changed the field. When asked why he chose glass as his medium of choice, he said this: *"There are only a few translucent materials on the planet that light can go through. I have always been attracted to the way light passes through glass."* Chihuly came on the glassblowing scene in 1971 and smashed every rule he encountered.

I chose these three individuals because of their persistence and determination to not let society grind them down and beat them into conformity. Everyone can be part of the crowd. It takes courage and guts to stand apart from it. These trailblazers not only carved their path; they also left markers for the rest of us to follow. Inspiration is everywhere; I found mine in a genius architect, a brilliant creative director, and an avant-garde, one-eyed glassblower.

21

WHEN CREATIVITY MEETS INSPIRED LEADERSHIP

In 1999, I got a job as an art director at Adams Outdoor Advertising, a billboard company with offices in fifteen markets. I was hired by the general manager of the Eastern Pennsylvania market, John Hayes. Hayes had decided that he needed to change the focus of the company from selling ad space on the side of the road to one that would champion creativity in every aspect of the company.

First, he was very clear to everyone about what the new mission would be. He gave me and the other art director full authority to reject what we deemed as poor designs. Second, he instituted weekly creative sessions to educate the account executives on basic design knowledge. *"In advertising, a better creative product will always be perceived as having more value and will generate more revenue than a less creative product. We were able to command higher prices than were being generated in much larger markets, and our creative*

L E S S O N S
LEARNED

A fear of failure must never be the reason that stops you from making the attempt.

product was the predominant reason," said Hayes. Creativity became a revered commodity. It was put on a pedestal. It was celebrated and used as a tool to drive revenue and attract top sales talent to join its workforce.

"People will work to a point for a paycheck. They will work harder for a leader they see as inspirational. But the highest performance level comes from people working for a vision that they see as good and noble. That vision becomes the reason that they get up in the morning, and it becomes the glue that binds the organization into a singular dynamic organism," Hayes adds.

I remember very clearly an incident when a client wanted to add their phone number to a design. Hayes said, *"No, we're not going to let them ruin what could be an amazing piece of outdoor advertising just because their corporate office says so."* The back and forth went on for weeks. It was clear to me that Hayes was not going to budge. He was willing to walk away from the sale. Think about that: he was willing to turn his back on a rather large sum of revenue simply because he refused to buckle on a core belief.

Once the customer realized Hayes wasn't going to blink, they approved the designs without the phone number. The client loved the designs once they were posted, and months later, the designs went on to win a national marketing award from the Outdoor Advertising Association of America. Hayes set the table for creative innovation to flourish.

Hayes core belief is that; *"Great leaders are able to develop a vision that people can buy into, and they are able to communicate the path that everyone needs to take to reach that vision. That is what needs to happen for an organization to become high achieving."*

LESSONS LEARNED

The daunting steps we avoid taking are always the ones that have the power to transform us the most.

22

THE HIDDEN POWER OF REJECTION

What is it about creativity that scares people? Why are new ideas usually met with resistance? Oscar Wilde once remarked, *"An idea that is not dangerous is not worthy of being called an idea at all."* I believe that an inherent bias against uncertainty and fear of the unknown are at the center of our trepidation when presented with a new idea. For work to be truly creative and groundbreaking, it must depart from the status quo of what is known or accepted, and that's what makes people uncomfortable.

Life is full of examples where ideas that were immediately rejected came to be accepted and celebrated years later. Alfred Wegener, a German polar researcher, geophysicist, and meteorologist, once theorized that the Earth's continents were moving apart very slowly and have been for millions of years. His theory of continental drift was soundly rejected by most other scientists. It was only in the 1960s that his approach finally became part of mainstream science. For a long time, his idea was considered preposterous.

LESSONS LEARNED

We've been programmed to avoid failure because of the criticism that follows it. Don't be fooled, it's the critics that carry all the fear.

If you are someone who works in a creative capacity, you will need to come to terms with the fact that you are going to hear phrases like "No, I don't think that is what we are looking for right now." It doesn't mean your idea isn't any good; it just means that they don't currently share your passion.

Whenever I present a new idea where I know the potential for rejection is high, I start out by sharing the origin of how the idea was created and developed. I will also give compelling reasons why I think the idea is sound and how it can evolve in the future.

Sometimes it works, sometimes it doesn't. But if, after a rejection, you can ask yourself, "What can I learn from this?" you create an opportunity to gain some wisdom. Ultimately, you get to choose how you proceed after a denial. You can either wallow in the pain of it or use it as fuel to go in another direction.

Consider J.K. Rowling, author of the wildly successful Harry Potter books. Before her first book got published, she had just lost her job, was almost broke, became recently divorced, and at one point fell into a deep depression while sitting on dozens of rejection letters for her unpublished manuscript about a boy wizard. She even admitted at one low point during the writing of the first book that she became so despondent she considered suicide.

Then, a small publishing house in London, Bloomsbury, took a chance on her story and published the first book, Harry Potter and the Philosopher's Stone, in 1997. Her series of seven books has since sold more than 450 million copies, won innumerable awards, been made into eight movies, and captivated millions of readers around the globe, thus transforming Rowling's life forever. If you remove the emotion from a rejection, you can harness the hidden power it contains. I won't try to sugarcoat it. Rejection sucks. But like most unpleasant experiences in life, if you can evaluate it and learn from it, you can move forward with renewed confidence.

23

LISTEN AND LEARN

believe most of us grow up hoping that one day, when we choose a profession, it's something that strikes a chord in our soul, permitting us to engage both our hearts and minds. That's especially the case for Lehigh Valley attorney, musician, and arts entrepreneur Bryan Tuk. If you assumed those professions don't have much in common, you'd be wrong. Tuk understands very well the business of modern life, and the twenty-four-hour-a-day connectivity in the digital age has dulled one of our senses to the point that it's now become a rare commodity: our ability to listen.

Too often when we are communicating with someone, we're not listening as much as we are waiting for our turn to speak, while possibly looking down at our phones or answering email. I think this is rude. Bryan agrees. *"Listening skills are the critical thread that runs through both playing in a band and running a business. The market can shift on you quickly, and you need to be able to spontaneously react to the changing conditions, which is what real musicians do when they play live."* If hearing is the physical ability, then listening is the skill. *"As musicians, the chief characteristic that will keep getting you hired is your ability to hear the band, the bass player, and the guitarist, so that the song you're playing sits together in the pocket, or if it's jazz, that the*

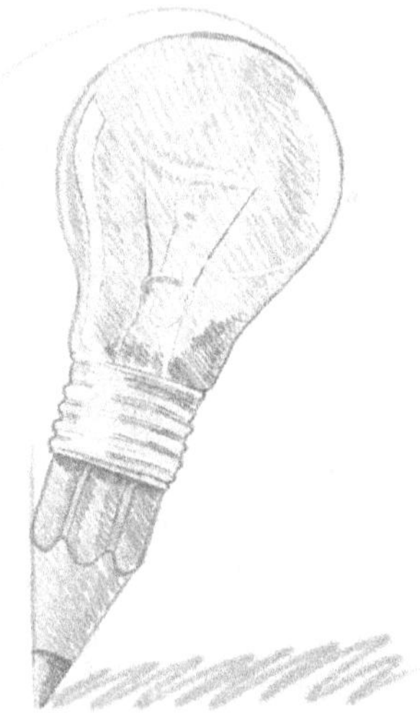

L E S S O N S
LEARNED

**Do work that feeds your
soul, not your ego.**

whole thing can transition with the ensemble going in the same direction," he adds.

Karl A. Menninger, one of the preeminent psychiatrists of the twentieth century, had this to say on the topic: *"Listening is a magnetic and strange thing, a creative force. The friends who listen to us are the ones we move toward. When we are listened to, it creates us, makes us unfold and expand."*

Listening also means paying attention not only to the story but how it is told, the use of language and voice, and how the other person uses his or her body to convey meaning. In other words, it means being aware of both verbal and non-verbal messages. These cues are extremely critical for Tuk in his law practice. To represent a client properly, an attorney needs to completely understand the challenges that clients face.

Tuk has clearly mastered the techniques that allow him to not only help his fellow artists and musicians in his law practice but also his bandmates when playing gigs to create smooth musical transitions or to pick up the slack for a less-experienced player.

Regardless of what stage he finds himself performing on, be it in the courtroom or the concert hall, he knows that while he'll always be appreciative of the applause following a rocking musical set, the real reward for him will always come from the client whose case he wins.

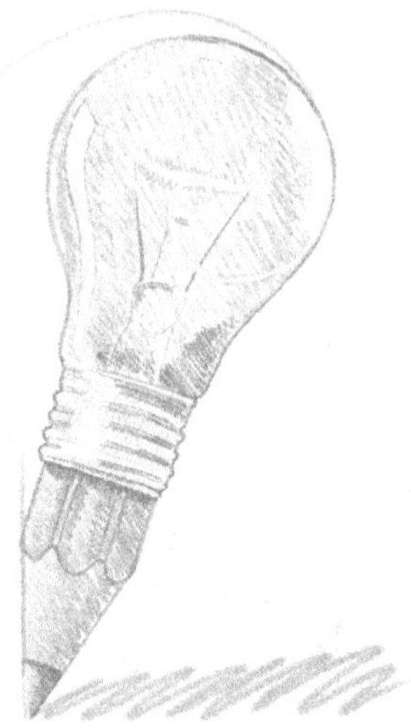

L E S S O N S
LEARNED

Real creativity in a corporate environment has a way of exposing bad leadership.

24

INNOVATION WILL NOT GROW IN A TOXIC ENVIRONMENT

Smart business owners today are always looking for new ways to attract top people to join their organizations. One of the best ways to accomplish this is to create a vibrant, creative and empowering workplace environment. As the workforce tightens and competition for exceptional workers intensifies, finding those candidates can prove challenging.

Margo Trott Collins, a creative marketing consultant, agrees. *"Every new addition to your team creates a new dynamic that will impact your workforce. The right person can move your company forward in new ways. They can and should have a positive influence in a way that grows your business, or at the very least maintain your success."*

In my career, I have experienced both. I've worked in environments where a healthy life/work balance was encouraged by the leadership, the work was creative and meaningful, and the employees were invited to take risks. I also have worked in toxic environments, and they will sap your energy, drain your soul, and make it difficult just to get through the day.

"I have seen time and time again how one or two bad hiring decisions can derail an entire workplace. I have also seen how a good hire can go bad quickly if the workplace is a toxic one. The best workplaces are innovative enough to evolve to meet the needs of the customers, the company, and the employees. Part of that 'secret sauce' is knowing how critical the right hire is for every position — and knowing how to keep them happy within the organization," Collins adds.

Having even one toxic person poisoning the culture inside your company can prove costly. *"The average cost-per-hire is over $4,100 and the average time it takes to fill a position is forty-two days, according to the Society for Human Resource Management's 2016 Human Capital Benchmarking Report. And the cost that making a bad hire can have on your company can be several tens of thousands of dollars,"* Collins cautions.

So, what does this all mean? Well, owners need to be open to set the conditions that create a culture where people cooperatively share their ideas, are not afraid to take risks, respect each other's contributions, and have autonomy to solve customer issues without involving management. If you're lucky enough to work in that type of environment, you will be more productive, have lower stress levels, and will look forward to going to work every day.

Consider this: have you ever found yourself getting anxious on a Sunday evening because you dread going into work the next day? That's a trauma response from your body telling you that you're unhappy with your job, and you should seek new employment.

"People are more interested than ever in company cultures and employer brands, even when they are not job hunting, which is why developing this is crucial to building a healthy workforce. Hiring someone who does not fit into your company culture can set up a climate of stress and distraction for everyone. And your talent will flee if there's too much negative drama," Collins emphasizes.

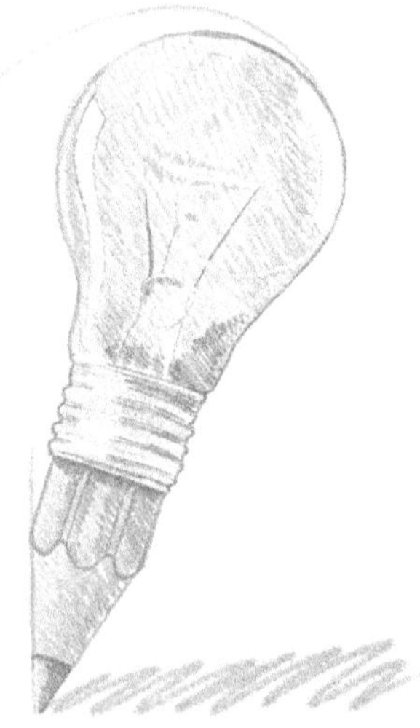

The best work happens when you feel your talents are celebrated, not merely tolerated.

25

FIVE TRUTHS I LEARNED THE HARD WAY

The world doesn't care if you love your job. The world owes you nothing, nor is it responsible for your happiness. That is why it's of critical importance to do work you are passionate about. Don't get into the habit of making excuses if your career doesn't go the way you planned. When you follow your passion, you tend to do good work. When you do good work, you will attract people who appreciate your talent and expertise. Do that consistently, and you'll never have to work a day in your life.

Sometimes, you can draw more inspiration from the people who don't believe in you than from the ones who do. I have always found it incredibly motivating when people would say to me that I can't do something. That's usually all the fuel I would need to put me on the road to accomplishing the goal. I had someone tell me once that I couldn't be a graphic designer because I didn't have a college degree. Oh, really? Thanks for the input; now watch as I work twice as hard as everyone else to prove you wrong.

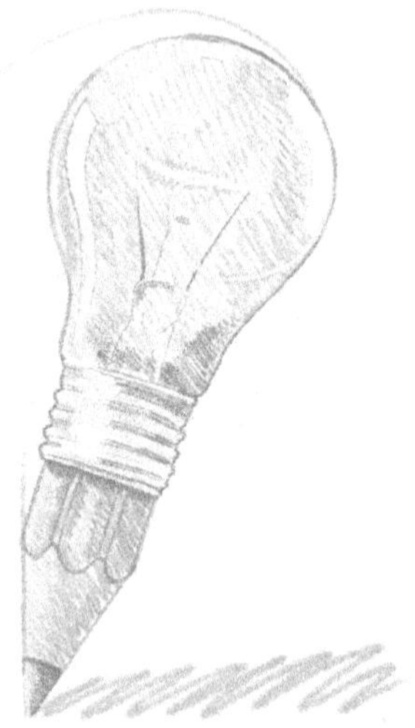

L E S S O N S
LEARNED

People who ridicule your dreams do so because they don't have the courage to fulfill their own.

You will need to fail before you can succeed. Failing at something is the only way to ever get better at it. Public speaking was something I always wanted to be able to do, but my first attempt was an unmitigated disaster. My voice cracked, I got cotton mouth, and I had trouble putting two coherent sentences together. The next time, my voice didn't break as much, I brought water to prevent my mouth from getting dry, and I had my thoughts organized on index cards. I learned from my previous attempt and made the necessary improvements to ensure it wouldn't happen again.

Stay humble. Humility can be a secret weapon to help you ward off the nasty effects of an overinflated ego. Approaching your work with humility opens you up to learning new techniques and skills that will help you get better at your craft. Nobody wants to work with someone who thinks they know everything. Don't let arrogance affect your attitude towards your job or your co-workers. Stay positive. Stay humble.

Never settle. You were born an original, don't die a copy. As much as we like to think of ourselves as individuals, the fact is that society too often encourages us to fit in, and that's how conformity takes over. The world isn't going to arrange itself to make your dreams come true. That's on you, and you won't be able to if every time you meet resistance, you buckle and go with the flow. Your job is to make sure you keep moving forward and weed out those people who would seek to derail your hopes and dreams and avoid them.

We all experience life differently. Our experiences growing up help to shape who we become and ultimately, how we view the world and our place in it. As you move through your career, always be open to making new mistakes and discovering your own universal truths.

L E S S O N S
LEARNED

A visionary leader never takes credit when things go right...but they are the first to accept responsibility when they don't.

26

COLLABORATION IS THE KEY TO UNLOCKING A BIG IDEA

As someone who has spent a significant portion of his professional career in pursuit of big ideas, it can often feel quixotic. The more time I spent working on idea generation, the more I learned that for a good idea to become a great idea, you need to be willing to collaborate. I experienced this firsthand when I worked with Dan Ross, the owner of R.M. Squared, an advertising agency that Ross started in 1992.

"I've always been a big believer in collaboration. It takes humility to show your idea to someone who may ultimately end up seeing something in it that you had not considered," Ross says. One of the lessons he taught me was to not fall in love with an idea too fast. Sometimes, you have to let it marinate overnight and look at it fresh in the morning.

The house rule inside the agency at the time was that it was okay to have a crappy day, but it was not okay to try and hide away and pretend that everything was all right. Ross would remind us that asking for help is not a sign of weakness; it's a sign of strength. Ross set the conditions at the agency for ideas to flow freely. He made sure that people felt supported to share their thoughts and opinions openly. That left an impact on me. The fact was he was willing to entertain different viewpoints, even if they differed from his own. A lot of business leaders are not ready to set up an environment that fosters that type of open, collaborative thought.

"In my years working in radio on WVUD in Dayton, Ohio, as an on-air talent, writing advertising copy as well as production, leadership at the station set a very high standard of what went out over the air, and everyone adhered to it," he says. Time and time again, he encouraged the staff to *"never settle"* and that *"good enough is not enough."* He permitted us to push our ideas out past our comfort zones. Which is a place Ross encouraged everyone to spend a lot of time visiting. That's because it's the place where he has discovered some of his most compelling, transformative thoughts.

"I also made sure never to judge a new idea too quickly. You'd be surprised how often you can uncover a good idea on the way back from a terrible one," Ross adds.

I remember one time struggling to write some radio ads for a college in Reading. Ross saw that I had grown frustrated attempting to write these commercials, so he offered this tip: *"Why don't you write a letter to yourself about how you would feel if you were about to make the leap from high school to college, and what that would feel like, and what your concerns would be?"* It worked. That insightful tip provided the spark I needed to complete the job.

Ross was the type of leader who took pride in helping his employees grow and learn. In fact, Ross often would lead by example when it came time to explore new client concepts. He often would demonstrate through his writing that no idea is too crazy. Albert Einstein understood this concept well: *"If at first the idea is not absurd, then there's no hope for it."* Don't be afraid to push your ideas into uncomfortable places. You just might be surprised by what you'll find there.

Working at R.M. Squared showed me that if a leader is willing to set the stage for creativity to receive proper respect, the ideas will show up. I was proud of the work that we produced. It was an experience whose lessons I have carried with me to this day because I got to participate in the thrill of taking ordinary ideas and turning them into extraordinary ones.

He was able to steer the company in a new direction. He changed the company's culture, and everything he hoped creativity would do for his clients, his employees, and the company came true. I got to experience what happens when the power of creativity meets inspiring leadership.

When you listen to your heart, engage your intellect, and chase your passion, you'll find your purpose.

27

TURNING THOUGHTS INTO IDEAS THAT HAVE VALUE

A recent study from Queen's University in Canada has discovered that the average person has over 6,000 thoughts per day. However, the study did not answer this: how many of those thoughts are original, creative, or unique? To that, I would add, of those 6,000 thoughts, how many have marketable value?

If you're someone who works in a creative capacity or is a manager whose role is evaluating other people's ideas, then you're aware of how challenging it can be to decide which ideas have real value.

I spend a large portion of my day thinking about solving marketing challenges, and when I get to a place where I feel like my ideas lack originality, I step back and regroup. John Hayes, former general manager of Adams Outdoor, an outdoor advertising company, believes this: *"People attribute higher product quality and value to any item that is creatively advertised. In the same way, they attribute higher intelligence to an individual who is capable of original thought."* I wish there were a better way to properly analyze good ideas and calculate their worth before their implementation. It's always a lot easier to assign value to an idea after it's successful. There's simply no way to know if a thought is any good or has value until somebody dares to bring it into existence. Unfortunately, nobody has a playbook containing the secret formulas for turning a good idea into a great one. The best way to test if an original thought has any value is to put it into action. I know that seems obvious, but far too often, when we overthink an idea and the possible results, analysis paralysis can set in, guaranteeing the idea will die. Overthinking can sap your confidence, drain your energy, and lead you down a path of fear and trepidation.

Creative people excel at putting ideas into action. Of course, they're acutely aware that not all their thoughts are going to be winners, but they're usually the ones who consistently show up with the courage to give one a go. I have the highest respect for people who willingly step into the arena and openly share their thoughts and ideas, knowing that they will be met with rejection nine times out of ten.

Matt Borrelli, a senior art director at Liquid, an Allentown-based agency focused on strategy, user experience design, digital marketing, and technology, agrees. *"It takes a brave person to present an original and untested thought. It also requires a certain amount of faith for a client to stake their brand's reputation in something new and unfamiliar. But great marketing results never start with safe ideas."*

The world is full of game-changing ideas that were once rejected when they were first presented. For example, imagine working at Western Union in 1876 and reading this internal memo stating, *"This 'telephone' has too many shortcomings to be seriously considered as a means of communication. Therefore, this device is of no value to us."* Ouch. Do you have any ideas you're sitting on, wondering if they're any good or have value? If yes, what's holding you back from using them? The journey to a win or loss starts on the same road, and action always beats intention.

So what's the way forward? Well, for one, we all have ideas. A good gauge for which one to breathe life into is the one you can't stop thinking about, the one that gnaws at you consistently by showing up in your daily thoughts. Don't be one of those people who go to their grave with their music still inside them. You owe it to yourself and the world to take the leap. I can promise you this: thinking about doing something will not help you overcome your fear; taking action will.

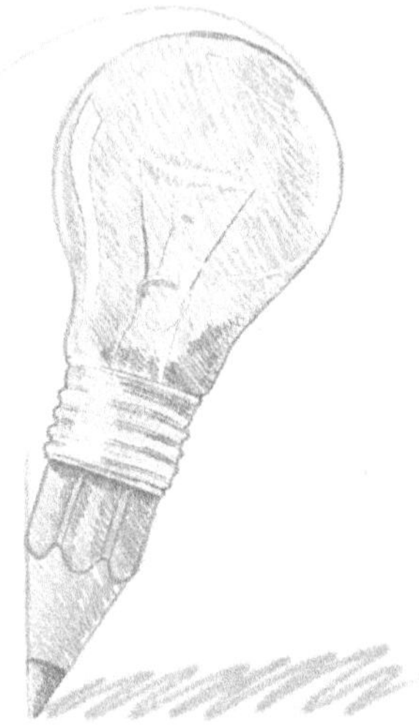

L E S S O N S
LEARNED

Leaders with high confidence levels excel at helping others rebuild theirs.

28

DEVELOPING AN ATTITUDE OF GRATITUDE

Back in the summer of 1983, I was working part-time at a sign company in Allentown. I was excited to start my career, and since I was already working at the company, I jumped at their offer of full-time employment. With my youthful exuberance, I was so eager to show the world what I had to offer that I didn't celebrate finishing high school, instead going immediately to work the day after graduation.

Six years into the role, the position began crashing down around me, forcing me to try and make sense of why it was happening. The business was doing well, but I was not. I had grown increasingly bitter and resentful and started blaming everyone and anything for what I perceived as a lack of opportunity. The problem wasn't the company; it was me.

My supervisor, Mr. Darryl Shellhamer, had witnessed my slow and steady transformation into the dark side, and he grew concerned. He spent time coaching me, often trying in vain to help me understand that my life was not as bad as I was making it out to be. He wanted me to stop looking for all the wrongs in every situation and instead focus my energies on the positive aspects. In retrospect, I can see what held me back was my complete lack of awareness and appreciation for all the good in my life. Privilege without gratitude becomes an entitlement, and entitlement is the natural enemy of gratefulness.

While a positive mental attitude was something that had eluded me during my time working with Schellhamer, his efforts were not in vain. Fast-forward some fifteen years later. I was working for a different company and had a rather rude awakening when I was asked to lead a team where several individuals needed major gratitude adjustments. That's when the lessons Schellhamer tried to teach me came full circle. Karma wanted my mea culpa. All that Schellhamer tried to instill in me I now found myself using to help my new team grow and succeed. Trust me when I say that I appreciated the irony. I now use the lessons taught to me that didn't stick then to help others change their behavior. The biggest lesson for me from Schellhamer was that he never gave up on me. He may have gotten frustrated, but he always believed that I had it within me to change. That left an impact on me.

Recent studies on the topic of gratitude have proven quite convincingly that many aspects of your life will improve once you begin embracing a positive mindset. Many people experience better sleep, less stress, improved relationships, lower blood pressure, more robust immune systems, and generally feel more alive, alert, and awake, and have higher optimism and happiness levels. Cultivating gratitude is not difficult. It merely requires that you shift your mental focus and be open to the abundance present in your life. The beauty of it is that anyone can do it, and the rewards are real and life-changing. Robert A. Emmons, Ph.D., a leading gratitude researcher, studied the link between gratitude and well-being. *"Gratitude is fertilizer for the mind, spreading connections and improving its function in nearly every realm of experience. Gratitude empowers us to take charge of our emotional lives and, as a consequence, our bodies reap the benefits."*

For the uninitiated, I'm sure this sounds like folly. I can assure you it's not. A positive mental mindset is one of the tools I use daily. Next time you find yourself spiraling down a rabbit hole of disappointment or feeling sorry for yourself or your current situation, try applying some good old-fashioned gratitude.

Over the years, whenever I'm asked about the one thing that helped me the most during any rough patches in my life or career, it always comes back to optimism. The singular ability to believe that whatever challenge you might find yourself facing, by being positive or looking for a silver lining, you can work your way through it. The Persian poet Rumi sums it up best: *"Wear gratitude like a coat, and it will feed every corner of your life."*

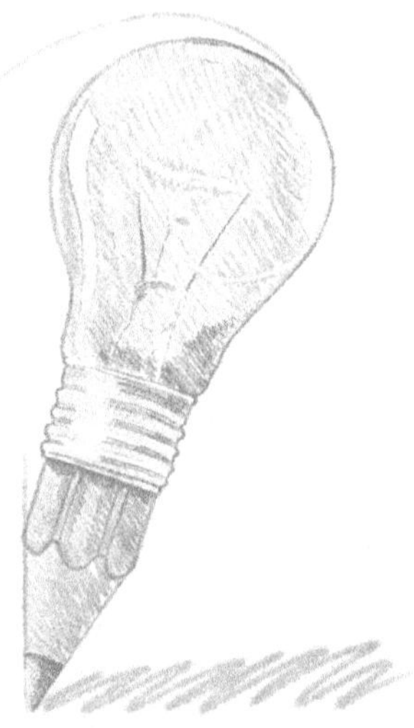

L E S S O N S
LEARNED

If you really want something, and you don't have the guts to ask for it, the answer will always be no.

Section 3: Creative Marketing

The advertising field has seen tremendous change in the past thirty years. Reaching an audience in today's over-communicated marketplace is challenging. The one thing that has not changed is how creativity gets used to help businesses cut through the clutter. Creativity, when applied and used correctly, can invigorate everything it touches. Far too many companies today do not know how to market themselves.

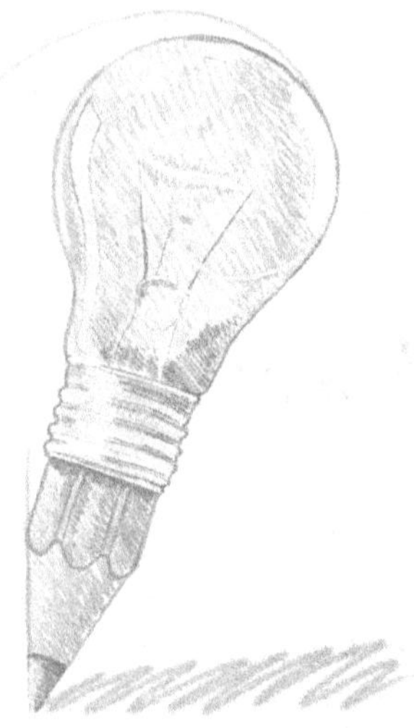

Great ideas can provoke great love or intense hate. It's when they inspire neither that you should worry.

29

5 WAYS COMPANIES CAN EMBRACE A CREATIVE CULTURE

I would have hoped that by now, business leaders would openly be using the transformative capability of creativity to invigorate their company culture. Instead, creativity remains widely misunderstood, and I find that confusing. Uninspired leaders may think that buying a couple of bean bag chairs or a foosball table for the company break room qualifies as a creative culture. Fortunately, creativity doesn't work that way. My educated guess is that creativity doesn't follow a predictable formula, making it challenging to track results, thus inspiring fear and trepidation in those who lack the courage to give it the proper status it deserves.

A creative culture starts at the top. An inspired leader is responsible for setting the overall tone inside the company, which, in turn, then has a significant influence on everyone else. If the culture is one of collaboration, trust, patience, and mutual respect, creativity can inspire people to want to learn and grow, ultimately leading to trackable results. A note of caution: if your sole reason for setting up a creative culture is to make more money, it'll fail fast. Money is an outcome, not a strategy. Money is essential to maintaining a healthy business, but it shouldn't influence every decision.

Here are five essential elements that you'll need to set up a creative culture. They all work together to set the conditions for creativity and innovation to flourish. You can't cherry-pick only the ones you like because you need them all.

1. Authenticity. It's the one element required if there's any hope of creating a culture where innovation will thrive and grow. Suppose management constantly reminds workers how they are not living up to their potential or that everyone needs to work harder, or they make staff feel uncomfortable. In any of those scenarios, the business will struggle to survive. That approach may have worked during the height of the Industrial Revolution, but not anymore. People today want to work for companies that value their commitment and dedication to their craft.

2. Vulnerability. There's nothing worse than a boss who thinks they have to have all the answers. The best leaders empower others to find solutions. Leaders who trust the people they hire will be amazed at how those individuals will rise to solve most challenges. Dr. Brené Brown said, *"To declare oneself 'not vulnerable' would be inauthentic and would leave a leader living in a perpetual state of denial and stress. So it's better and more courageous for every leader to acknowledge the fact that vulnerability is there."*

3. Risk. One of the absolute worst things a leader can do is stigmatize mistakes. Everyone makes mistakes. It's an integral part of the process of looking for big ideas. Not every idea is going to work, and that's okay. Success and failure are not opposites; they are two sides of the same coin. Some of the world's most significant discoveries happened due to unintended outcomes. The wheel, the printing press, Post-it notes, the microwave oven, penicillin, Teflon, and Play-Doh were all created by accident while their inventors worked on a different problem. Creativity will not prosper in an organization if everyone is terrified of making a mistake. British comedy legend and Monty Python member John Cleese agrees. *"Nothing will stop you from being creative more effectively as the fear of making mistakes."* A leader who allows people to risk being wrong understands that mistakes can often stimulate a better idea.

4. Flexibility. A crucial element in creating the right conditions in a creative culture, flexibility allows managers to try new approaches. Flexibility breeds innovation and a sense of excitement within the organization. People do their best when empowered and encouraged to seek new alternatives to issues and challenges without fear of reprisals. In any worthwhile business endeavor, it's important to remain steadfast in the mission but flexible in the approach. Business author and management consultant Tom Peters sums up flexibility like this: *"Life is pretty simple: You do some stuff. Most fails. Some works. You do more of what works. If it works big, others quickly copy it. Then you do something else. The trick is the doing something else."*

5. Diversity. Our differences will always make us unique. If everyone is looking at a problem from the same perspective, no new insights will emerge. In problem-solving, it's essential to know that ideas can come from anyone. A diverse environment will go a long way in helping people look at problems from multiple angles. Try not to put people in silos. Value everyone's thoughts and opinions because the more the team openly contributes, the odds of solving the challenge increase exponentially. Stephen R. Covey, the author of The 7 Habits of Highly Effective People, said,

"Seek first to understand, then to be understood." While this may all seem like common sense advice, too many business leaders are not willing to invest in the creative health of their employees. In 2014, Forrester Consulting was asked by Adobe® to quantify and qualify just how creativity impacts business results. The study's outcome was surprising; they discovered that companies that embrace a creative culture outperform peers and competitors on many key business performance indicators, including revenue growth, market share, and talent acquisition.

I've outlined just five of the elements that go into building a healthy, creative culture. All five elements were present in the best companies I've worked for. So, yes, it's a process that requires everyone's full participation, but one where the benefits far outweigh the risks.

30

WHY MENTORS MATTER MORE THAN EVER

I'm hoping this will not come as a shock to you, but it's rare that we succeed in life or business without any outside influence or help along the way. All of us can benefit from having positive role models or mentors in our lives. The outstanding ones will provide guidance, much-needed instruction, and, when appropriate, a little tough love. I was fortunate to have had exceptional mentors growing up who inspired me, guided me, challenged me, and often told me the things that I needed to hear, not necessarily what I wanted to hear.

The people who mentored me provided valuable lessons that, to this day, I still call upon when things in my life become challenging. I believe there's no more noble calling than to provide fundamental insight to someone looking for guidance to help them maximize their potential. A good mentoring relationship can last a lifetime or only a few short months; what ultimately matters is the wisdom and lessons that are imparted. Great mentors see the talent and ability within you long before seeing it in yourself.

LESSONS LEARNED

Don't judge your success
by how much money
you'll make, judge it by the
difference you'll make.

"Show me a successful individual, and I'll show you someone who had real positive influences in their life. I don't care what you do for a living—if you do it well, I'm sure someone was cheering you on or showing the way," said Academy Award-winning actor Denzel Washington.

I have tried to pay it forward and positively influence the people I've encountered on my journey through life and the places I've worked. To this day, I enjoy helping people, and I am not shy about openly expressing my opinions, knowledge, or life lessons when asked.

Mentors are everywhere; it's finding a good one that can prove challenging. Parents, teachers, coaches, and co-workers are all uniquely positioned to impart positive knowledge. However, to be an effective mentor, you need to be authentic, trustworthy, and above all, be willing to invest in others without expecting anything in return. When you freely give your time, energy, and guidance to someone who appreciates it, you'll discover that you'll be transformed through the process as well.

Kimberly Hopkins, former executive director of the Wilson Area Partners in Education Foundation (Easton, PA), believes that *"Mentorship doesn't have to be complicated. The most impactful gift a mentor can impart, for both children and adults, is an ear to listen without judgment. When someone feels heard, they also feel valued. Over time, this simple gift can empower a mentee to pursue options and opportunities that might otherwise have seemed impossible."*

My favorite story about making a life-changing impact is about an older gentleman taking his dog for a morning walk on a lonely beach. As he's walking, he sees in the distance the shape of what looks to be a person picking something up and then lobbing it into the sea. As the man gets closer, he's able to see the thousands of starfish that have beached themselves on the sand and will die if they don't get help. He feels compelled to ask a question. *"Hey, what are you doing?"* A young man responds, *"I'm throwing these starfish back into the sea so they will survive; otherwise, they won't make it."* The older man responds with a confused look on his face, laughs and says, *"There are simply too many of them; it's a noble gesture, but you can't possibly make a difference."*

At that moment, the young man bends down, picks up a starfish, and casually tosses it back into the sea while turning to the older gentleman, saying,

"Well, I made a difference to that one."

31

ALL BUSINESS IS PERSONAL

There's a saying that's used when describing any type of business interaction when the other party ends up being disappointed: "Hey, it's not personal; it's just business." It sounds to me like an excuse for treating people poorly. Everything is personal, from how we treat each other in social situations to how we conduct ourselves when doing business transactions.

That insensitive saying should be erased from the lexicon and replaced with training for managers on improving their emotional intelligence. While I understand that not "taking it personally" is a way to protect oneself from disappointment and rejection, someone who takes their work "personally" is more loyal and dedicated to their job.

The American Psychological Association defines Emotional Intelligence (EQ) as a type of intelligence that involves the ability to process emotional information and use it in reasoning and other cognitive activities.

That definition might scare some managers because the old-school model was to leave your emotions out of any decision-making process. Yet, studies have consistently shown that emotional intelligence accounts for roughly 90% of the traits a leader needs to run a company effectively. There's a seismic shift occurring in how businesses are starting to communicate and treat their employees. Between the great resignation and quiet quitting, companies realize that this issue needs addressing, or they must face the added costs of finding and retaining quality employees. Employee retention starts with building a positive communication culture inside a company.

Sure, all the perks presently making the rounds at various companies are excellent. Still, there's nothing better than when you work at a company where the leadership understands and employs emotional intelligence. If leaders understand how to use EQ, the benefits far outweigh the risks. For example, leaders with high levels of EQ are great listeners, show empathy, make better decisions, keep their cool under pressure, embrace change, and strongly consider how their choices will affect everyone, not just the bottom line.

Conversely, managers with low EQ often blame others for poor results, refuse to take responsibility when things go wrong, can be overly critical of others, and have aggressive communication styles. A high EQ is something that a good hiring manager will look for when filling open positions., because those individuals are better at managing conflict, excel at problem-solving, and are comfortable with change. Not because they believe they have all the answers but rather because their ego does not lead them. They tend to be open to new ideas and work toward finding positive solutions, all while avoiding office drama. These people find motivation when their passion meets their purpose. Money, title, and acclaim do not drive the high-EQ individual. One of the top three reasons employees cited for changing jobs in 2021 was "feeling disrespected." The other two were low pay and lack of opportunity within the organization.

Managers must consider how financially damaging it can be when a dedicated, passionate, loyal employee leaves the company. According to Glassdoor, the average company spends about $4,000 to hire a new employee, often taking around fifty days to fill the position. That might not sound like much, but there are other hidden costs, too, like how employee morale suffers when good people start leaving with more frequency.

Here are some simple tips to increase your EQ immediately. First, stop thinking that you have to have all the answers. Make an effort to listen more and talk less. Be willing to accept criticism without feeling the need to defend yourself. Be more introspective. Don't stigmatize mistakes. Try and see things from different perspectives. And above all, stop saying, "It's not personal, it's just business."

LESSONS LEARNED

The best advice comes from those who have internalized a valuable lesson by way of a life-altering experience.

32

THE NOW ECONOMY MEANS BUSINESS

So, what exactly is the NOW economy? John Dodds, senior member of The Sharp End, a branding and marketing strategy consultancy based in the Lehigh Valley, describes it like this: *"The NOW economy is one where the consumer wants individualized experiences from the brand. In that ecosystem, consumers drive the demand, and in many ways, whether or not the brand stays relevant."* Dodds helps organizations identify and communicate their uniqueness to the market in both the B2C and B2B sectors and works to guide companies as they navigate their way through this brave new marketing world.

Author and motivational speaker Steve Maraboli believes this: *"When companies replace a sense of service and gratitude with a sense of entitlement and expectation, we quickly see the demise of the relationship, society, and the economy."* Which is why one of the biggest threats the NOW economy exposes is that companies with bad internal politics and a weak organizational structure refuse to support new ideas, often stifling any innovation and creativity.

Technology expert Ken Goldstein offers this: *"Creativity tempered by sound judgment is the currency of the NOW economy. It remains largely an open playing field for anyone who wants to relearn on a daily basis everything they thought they knew."* British author and advertising guru Sir John Hegarty agrees. "Without a passion for what you're producing, you may well be able to manage a business, but you will never be able to inspire greatness."

A recent example of that model in action is suitcase manufacturer AWAY founded by former Warby Parker executives Steph Korey and Jennifer Rubio in 2015. The origin story of the brand is a simple one. Cofounder Jen Rubio's suitcase broke on a trip to Switzerland, and she struggled to find a replacement. She sent text messages to her well-traveled friends, hoping at least one could provide a usable suggestion, but none did.

The pair saw an opening in the suitcase market and went to work creating an affordable, durable hard-shell suitcase with wheels and a built-in battery pack for charging electronics. *"They built the brand through the quality of the product and the ease at which consumers can interact with them online. AWAY drove awareness through their social media channels, which allowed consumers to share their travel stories and love of the AWAY product,"* Dodds adds.

Successful business leaders instinctively know that industry disruption will continue to accelerate with technology and innovation being the only path to competitive differentiation.

"It doesn't matter if you're large or small, every company needs a balance of humanity and technology. Humanity works with the customer's overall experience with the brand, and technology is there to ensure everything on

the back end runs smoothly. These elements can help you build a strong brand, but you can't do it reactively or incrementally; you need a clear vision," Dodds stresses. Tech-savvy consumers award brand loyalty to companies that deliver innovative, personalized services that focus on positive brand experiences. While he acknowledges that the NOW economy puts consumers in the driver's seat, he believes that the future will be all about voice. Voice search, voice command, voice knowledge, voice information. In many ways, it's already here. *"The NOW economy will become the future economy, and voice will be at the forefront of how we get our knowledge, how we order things, how we entertain ourselves. Voice will be the new search,"* Dodds says.

It's going to be fascinating to watch how this all unfolds in the coming years. B2B organizations must adapt to the NOW economy and recognize the impact that it will have on its processes and customer relationships. It also doesn't matter if you call this period the "sharing economy" or the "NOW economy," it's here to stay, and it means business.

L E S S O N S
LEARNED

Surround yourself with people who will tell you what you need to hear, not what you want to hear.

33

LIFE LESSONS FROM THE GAME OF GOLF

The average American spends approximately forty-three years of their life working before they retire. So, my question is this: why would anyone want to work doing something they aren't passionate about? I believe it's important you spend your working life doing something that resonates deep within your soul. Enter Mary Lengle of New Tripoli, PA. She grew up learning about the game of golf through a grandfather who instilled in her that golf is a game that brings people together. Lengle didn't realize at the time what the impact of those childhood talks would mean to her until many years later.

Early in her career, she worked at Rodale Inc. in the book division, working with the likes of Denise Austin, Gary Player, LL Cool J, Morgan Freeman, and renowned chef Jacques Pépin, helping them promote their respective books. While she enjoyed the work, she knew deep down that if she were ever to find real satisfaction in her career, she would need to find a way to combine her love of golf and storytelling abilities. *We spend so much of our lives waiting for permission. In school, you need permission from teachers, and in the workplace, you need permission from a boss before trying out a* new idea. *You just reach a point where you realize that you don't need anyone's permission anymore because it stifles your creativity and opportunities,"* says Lengle.

In 2016, she was done asking for permission. She knew it was time to finally combine those passions by teaming up with PGA professional and local golf instructor Eric Cogorno to build his business beyond just individual coaching. *"As I worked with Eric on my golf game, I saw how he collaborated with other students, and what I saw was unique and special, especially in his instruction with the junior golfers. A level of expertise and passion on par with other talent and brands I've worked with in my PR and production career,"* Lengle observes.

Lengle is working to become an ambassador for the game of golf by producing content that she hopes golfers of any age will find compelling and useful. It's a simple premise, but it's one that, for her, provides meaning and impact to her life. They don't have a road map for how they're going to get there, and they're okay with that. "Eric and I believe in what we are doing, and we know that our initial concept may evolve, and that's okay because that's how you set the conditions for innovation to happen," Lengle adds. She and Cogorno are in the phase of their plan where most business leaders would start getting nervous because they want to see that quick return on the investment. Lengle is comfortable with being uncomfortable, and golf provides all the motivation she needs.

"Golf is a game where you must learn to detach from the outcome. You can't focus on the past; you must stay present and in the moment and deal with the constantly changing variables that exist every time you step up to the tee." Not only is that great advice for golf, but it's an excellent way to approach your life.

Lengle can accept that not everyone will understand her mission. But what she does know is, when it comes to your business or personal life, if you're going to take a risk where failure is possible, then you'd better be doing something you love because that's ultimately how you'll succeed.

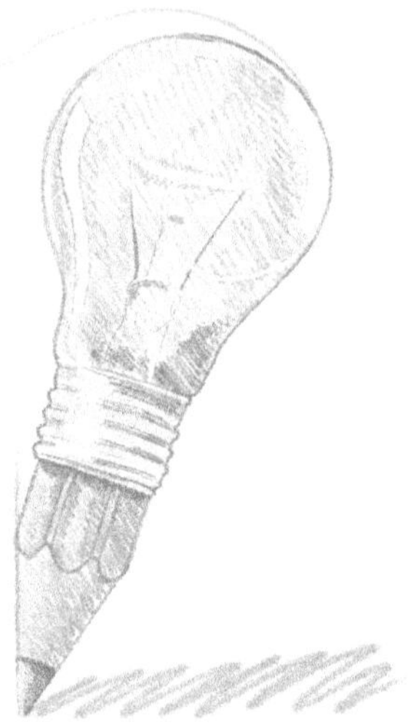

LESSONS
LEARNED

A transformative idea will often reveal itself to you during a time when you are least ready to acknowledge it.

34

DO NOT SETTLE FOR ACCEPTABLE, PUSH FOR EXCEPTIONAL

In 2004, I was working as a creative director for an advertising agency called R.M. Squared. One of our clients was Plantique, a high-end landscaping company. We were asked by the president at that time, Michael McShane, if we could come up with something in support of the company's decision to become a sponsor of Musikfest that year. I remember thinking that whatever we came up with should be something that would entertain as well as inform.

I also believed that people who were there to see a show would react more positively if the commercial blended those two elements seamlessly. From those insights, an idea sprouted.

I happened to casually mention one day to John Mulder, the production director, that I thought it would be cool if Robert Plant, former lead singer of the rock band Led Zeppelin, would play Musikfest, which would make Plantique the obvious choice to sponsor that show.

The next day, when John came in, the sly smile on his face told me he had something interesting to share. "Read this," he said. He handed me a sheet of paper, and on it was a list of the musicians and bands that had a connection to nature. Michelle Branch, Buddy Holly, Soundgarden, the Rolling Stones, Guns N' Roses, and, of course, Robert Plant. All it needed was a way to tie it all together. I gathered the team, and we started the process. After some serious investment in time coming up with taglines, it began to feel like we hit a wall. The connection to the band names and the Plantique name was established; what was not so clear was how to tie the whole concept back to Musikfest.

As frustration began to creep into the process, I remembered a quote from Bob Kuperman, former president and CEO of DDB, who spent over forty years working in a creative capacity: *"Don't settle for the acceptable idea; always push for the more exceptional one."* Easier said than done, but we kept pushing forward. After several hours, I was ready to put an end to it when Tony Zaino, one of the editors, out of complete frustration, blurted out, "It's like music is in their nature, and great landscaping is in Plantique's." That's what was missing.

The package now had a bow on it. The extra time had paid off. The finished spot used the names set against a black background with the first name of the artist or band in white and the other half in green. A hard-driving music track was used to emphasize each name as it appeared on the screen. The end screen had the text Music is in their nature, great landscaping is in ours. Simple yet powerful.

McShane remembers seeing the spot for the first time. *"The beauty of the ad was that it blended the brand seamlessly with the messaging, venue, and demographic that viewed it. Our clients loved the creativity and how we delivered our tagline through music."*

The whole experience taught me that when it comes to big ideas, you must be willing to put the time in and let the process work and not let frustration dampen your enthusiasm as you search for your big idea. Yes, good ideas can happen quickly; it's the exceptional ones that take a little longer.

People excel in work environments where they are empowered and encouraged to take risks.

35

PASSION YOU CAN TASTE

The Lehigh Valley is indeed known for its ability to produce award-winning products. One of the products in our area that has received notable accolades over the years is wine. Winemaking is a process that relies on both science and art. You can spend decades learning everything there is to know about the craft, but if you leave out the art, you risk mediocrity.

Jim Hutchings, a wine advisor who works in the tasting room and gives tours of the vineyards at Vynecrest, one of the oldest vineyards in the area, agrees. *"Much like a musician must know the technical aspects as well as the emotional, wine needs a solid understanding of both. Wine can be technically perfect, but without emotion, it will be flat. Likewise, a wine that has passion can also be flawed yet still enjoyable."*

Jim spends his days as a client engagement manager at Trifecta helping enterprise-level customers with their technology, but he loves being around the process of making wine because it allows him to embrace his creative side. *"Working with technology all day almost requires a hobby that permits the exploration of passion. Wine lets me embrace my creative side,"* Hutchings adds.

Then there's Austrian-born pianist Artur Schnabel, one of the world's most intellectually intense musicians, who said this about his playing: *"The notes I handle no better than many pianists. But the pauses between the notes – ah, that is where the art resides."* Anyone looking to take their skills to a new level needs to know how to work their pauses. You could be making furniture, writing a song, creating a marketing campaign, acting in a play, or working in the culinary arts, and you should know where your art "resides" if you desire to create something worthy of people's respect and admiration.

In 2008, the Lehigh Valley received the designation of being an American Viticultural Area, which means we're a recognized wine-producing region. For Jim, he's on a constant quest to find the pauses between the notes. *"I love how wine evolves. I love how the same wine can be uniquely different each time you try it and how the same grapes from the same vineyard can produce an entirely different wine if handled differently or compared from season to season. I love its breadth across regions, grapes, and vintages and the depth that a single wine may possess, evolving on the palate and lingering with us well after that final swallow."* With eight vineyards currently operating and producing a variety of great wines right here in the Lehigh Valley, you have plenty of opportunities to find and taste the one that fits you.

Hutchings offers this advice to anyone looking to improve their palette: *"Work on fine-tuning your sense of smell. Make a concerted effort to smell the shavings when you sharpen a pencil, smell the wet sidewalk after a summer thunderstorm. Smell the fresh-cut grass or a pepper from the garden. Smell the forest floor when you go on a hike through the woods. Take note of the individual components and then marvel when you can dissect a wine and experience many of the same scents and tastes."*

Wine is a product that's made with love, passion, and science. Love is not only something you experience; it's also something you can taste.

L E S S O N S
LEARNED

If you remove emotion from a rejection, you can harness the hidden power it contains.

36

STEVE VENGROVE IS THE REEL DEAL

In fly-fishing, it's incredibly challenging to land a fly in just the right location to entice a fish to strike. Steve Vengrove, who's spent his career catching big ideas for some of the world's largest brands as an executive creative director/member of the board of directors for Saatchi & Saatchi, understands this very well. *"Fishing and idea-generating can sometimes be elusive experiences. You must be willing to invest the time because both are highly specialized activities that require large amounts of patience. They also happen to be the only two things I'm good at,"* jokes Vengrove. He once responded to an ad for a copywriter posted for the agency Dancer Fitzgerald Sample (DFS) by sending this risky response to their creative director, Jack Keil: *"I would like to work for you because I believe that every ad agency should have a fly fisherman on its staff."* He sent no resume, included no samples of his work. The plan paid off. After an interview with Jack, he landed the job. In 1986, Saatchi & Saatchi purchased DFS. Today, Saatchi is still one of the largest global communications agencies, with over 140 offices in 76 countries and more than 6,500 workers around the world. Steve spent close to sixteen years working alongside some of the most prominent brands in the world, including Toyota, Procter & Gamble, General Mills, and Wendy's.

Jack Smart, a creative director who worked with Steve at DFS and Saatchi, says this about working with him: *"Steve always had a clown nose in his pocket and would put it on in a restaurant, his office, or in a meeting. Working for Steve wasn't work; it was clown noses, jokes, funny commercials, and very happy, successful clients."* Jack and his team were responsible for creating the wildly successful "Oh, what a feeling!" Toyota automotive campaign featuring people jumping in slow motion over their excitement of owning a Toyota. Another successful campaign Steve had a hand in was "Cuckoo for Cocoa Puffs," featuring "Sonny" the cuckoo bird, who goes crazy every time he tastes the chocolaty cereal. Steve understood how to navigate the waters of the agency world. *"I was lucky in that I was able to surround myself with people who were better than me. That's what made the difference. I always worked with really talented people. Many times, I would come up with the initial idea, and I always counted on my team to find ways to make it better, and they would."*

Saatchi once had the opportunity to present a new concept to Wendy's. The agency was in the process of acquiring the rights to the song "Georgia on My Mind," and after reworking some of the lyrics, Steve hired jazz musician Grady Tate to rerecord the song as 'Wendy's on My Mind.' *"It was such a strong idea that I believe had they bought it, it would have sold them a lot of hamburgers,"* says Vengrove. Even though this idea was *"the one that got away,"* he keeps it in perspective. He's proud of the people he has mentored over the years, his lifelong agency friendships, and the work he did on behalf of Saatchi and DFS's clients.

Since retiring to Bethlehem, Vengrove no longer has to worry about catching his next big idea. He now pours his creative energy into getting the Saucon Creek trout to bite his hand-tied flies. He's happy with the ideas he caught while working for Saatchi. Now, he's at peace with releasing what he catches.

157

L E S S O N S
LEARNED

Leadership is serventhood. It's the ability to place the needs of others above your own.

37

LOOK OUTSIDE YOUR OWN INDUSTRY TO DISRUPT IT

In 2017, I attended the Sharing Summit on the campus of Lehigh University at Iacocca Hall. The event was a gathering of business owners and entrepreneurs to discuss the transition from the industrial economy to the sharing economy. The keynote speech was given by Jeff Hoffman, co-founder of Priceline.

He spoke on a variety of interesting topics, but there were two that really captivated me. He told us about an exercise he does every morning called "info-sponging." He spends up to twenty minutes a day reading about something he's curious about. It could be from a newspaper, book, website, or magazine article.

It's the one time of day where he's trying to soak up as much new information as he possibly can. The trick to this daily ritual is that the topics he chooses are not directly related to anything he's currently involved in or working on. The whole point of the exercise is that he reads material or topics that he has no obvious connection to. Hoffman believes that the key to success is to have a broader funnel and to always be passionately curious. That's what will set you apart. The second item he shared that drew me in was that he believes that anyone looking to disrupt the industry they work in cannot do so from the inside. In other words, if you work in healthcare, you must look outside your own industry for innovation. *"If you work in healthcare, what do you work on all day long? Healthcare,"* Hoffman says. *"What problems do you solve all day? Healthcare problems. If I said to you, 'Hey, I'm going to the banking industry conference, do you want to go?' You might say, 'No, I don't do banking. I'm in healthcare."*

Uber was never going to be created by a taxi company, and Airbnb was never going to be coaxed into existence by a hotel chain. But those businesses have completely disrupted their respective industries.

History has shown examples of this theory in action. Archimedes, in the original "eureka" moment, discovered a method for measuring the volume of an irregularly shaped object in relationship to the gold in the king's crown while he took a bath. Gutenberg is widely credited with combining the idea of block printing (which the Chinese had been using since the eleventh century) with a screw press that was mainly used for olive oil and wine production and brought printing to the masses with his Gutenberg Bible.

So, what problems or business challenges could you be solving by looking at other industries for the answer? It again comes down to getting out of your own way and being willing to expand your comfort zone. Maybe you should add info-sponging into your daily ritual. You don't have to have all the answers; you just have to be ready to take action when your "eureka" moment happens.

38

THE MAN WHO INVENTED THE TWENTIETH CENTURY

Imagine being the person who was so plugged into the workings of our universe that he was regarded in some circles as having invented the twentieth century. The inventions this person created over his eighty-seven years on the planet, particularly in the late 1800s, are the basis for much of our modern lifestyle. You may have heard of his discoveries. The radio, fluorescent lighting, the electric motor, remote control, radar, neon lighting, X-rays, wireless communications; he even built the first hydroelectric plant at Niagara Falls to prove that water could be used as a practical energy source. He was the first person to record radio waves coming from deep space, thus ushering in the field of radio astronomy.

His name was Nikola Tesla, and he was a man ahead of his time. He held four doctorate degrees: philosophy, physics, electrical engineering, and mechanical engineering, and possessed an IQ of 200. In 1898, he submitted the patent for a radio-controlled robot boat

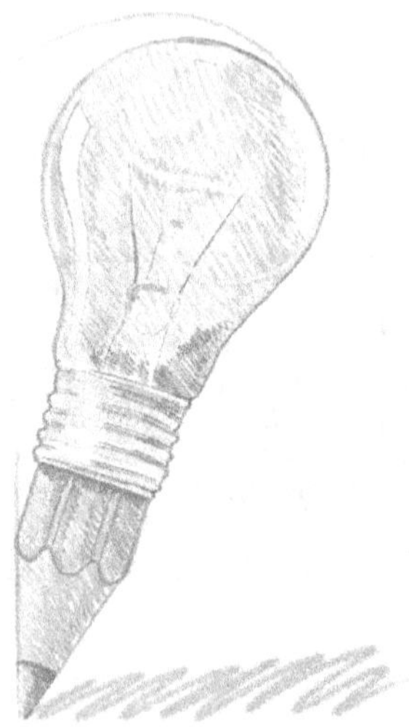

L E S S O N S
LEARNED

A moral bankruptcy exists when you judge someone's happiness based on their net worth.

that, when placed in water, could be maneuvered without any visible connection between boat and operator because it functioned on radio waves. In 1901, Italian inventor Guglielmo Marconi claimed all the first patents for radio from plans originally developed by Tesla. It wasn't until sixty-four years later, after both men were deceased (Tesla having died in 1943), that the U.S. Supreme Court ruled that all of Marconi's radio patents were invalid and awarded them to Tesla's estate.

Tesla also worked on a way to develop a global system of giant radio towers that would wirelessly relay news, stock reports, pictures, and even free electricity for one and all. J.P. Morgan, one of the world's most powerful bankers of his era, who financed railroads and helped organize U.S. Steel and General Electric, found out that there would be no way to regulate or make money from it, so he pulled his funding and gave it to Thomas Edison. I believe that Tesla's inventions pushed people way outside of their comfort zones and his discoveries frightened and confused people, which undoubtedly contributed to his reclusiveness.

Tesla died broke and alone, other than for some pigeons he befriended, on the thirty-third floor in room 3327 of the New Yorker Hotel in New York City. He never married, and he never had any children. He focused every ounce of his energy on his work. My hope is that future generations will come to know the man for more than just being the namesake of Elon Musk's electric car company.

The fact that Tesla does not have a functioning United States museum honoring him bothers me greatly. However, plans have been underway for several years in Shoreham, New York, at the site of Tesla's last remaining U.S. laboratory named 'Wardenclyffe.' Recently, the building suffered a devastating fire, which has pushed back plans to restore the laboratory into a global science center. According to a press release at www.teslasciencecenter.org, Tesla Science Center Executive Director Marc Alessi stated, *"It brings a sense of relief to share that the structural integrity of the building, dating back to 1901, seems to have withstood the ordeal. For ongoing updates and verified information, please visit our website at www.teslasciencecenter.org. Together, we will navigate this crisis and emerge stronger, honoring the legacy of Nikola Tesla and the spirit of innovation, determination, and resiliency that this center embodies."*

Tesla was a genius and a visionary, and he had a clear understanding of what his ultimate legacy would be when he said, *"Let the future tell the truth, and evaluate each one according to his work and accomplishments. The present is theirs; the future, for which I have worked, is mine."*

39

WHERE CREATIVITY TAKES CENTER STAGE

Of all the many ways businesses can use creativity, there's probably no greater example than Civic Theatre in the west end of Allentown. The creative spirit is alive and well due in large part to the man who's been its artistic director for the past twenty years, William Sanders.

Q: How much of a role does creativity play in a theater production?

Everything about a theater production is creativity. You might say creativity is the star of the production. The director, the designers, the book writer, the composer, the lyricist, the playwright...everyone behind the scenes is actually referred to as "creatives," as in "cast and creatives."

Q: What does your creativity mean to you?

A: Creativity has always been such a part of my life that I don't really know where I would be without it. It certainly

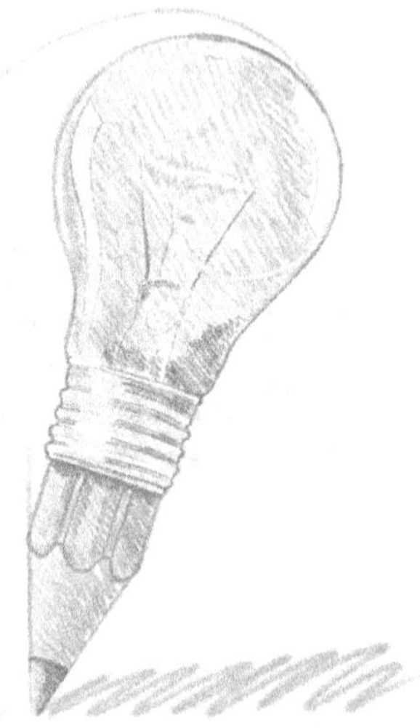

LESSONS LEARNED

Failure and success need each other. They are two sides of the same coin.

has made me make my way in life. After directing my first musical in fourth grade, I adapted TV shows and movies all through grade school and middle school. I've always loved painting pictures and creating pretty pictures on stage. So my creativity means everything to me. It is, for want of a better word, my life. Wow. Never really thought of that before.

Q: What do you love about being an artistic director at Civic Theatre?

A: What I love about my job and my chosen path is the collaboration with people of so many different experience levels. There's very rarely any jockeying for position or diva trips or unkindness. Unfortunately, I think sometimes creativity and imagination go hand in hand with sensitivity. And I have very thin skin. That doesn't always bode well for ambition in the arts. So I'm very lucky to have been able to, as a friend recently told me, follow my heart. I also love that I get to sometimes bring work to the area that otherwise may not be seen and to have the opportunity to do the work in such a glorious old theater.

Q: If you had to do it all over again, would you choose the same career path?

A: Absolutely. I definitely miss...Or I think I miss... Acting. But I couldn't imagine my life without being an actor/dancer, then a director/choreographer. It has been...I'm getting emotional...extremely rewarding and I've been so lucky.

Q: What advice would you give a young person looking to go in to acting?

A: This is going to sound so cliché, but it was said to me: you have to love it beyond everything else and you have to be prepared to not make a living. See as much theater as possible. See great actors doing Shakespeare. See the best people you possibly can. Study, train, read all the books, make sure it's your passion, and then, when you get those opportunities to act, forget it all and just use your imagination and jump into the world of the play.

Q: What's the one thing you wish you knew when you were starting out?

A: That I should've gone to therapy much younger. I wish that I had known that it's really about confidence. I may sound like Maria in The Sound of Music, but it's true. I was bullied as a kid, and I didn't realize until quite recently how much that made me need people's approval. "Like me. Like me. Like me." And what that did was whittle away at my self-confidence. That's another thing I love about Civic; it was a place that eventually felt like home, and one is always confident at home. If I were starting again, I would definitely do everything I could to learn and cultivate self-reliance and confidence.

Q: Can you name an instance where creativity was used to enhance a production?

A: There are so many instances. I can't realistically answer that question because with what we do, creativity is the locus of it. One of my favorite creative moments was coming up with the ending of Christmas Carol. My friend Sharon (Civic's fearless leader for decades) had written a script that I was tweaking to direct in 1989, and I was retyping it on the old Olivetti in our old box office on 19th Street. The storyteller was finishing his speech, and I had an idea. I still remember excitedly calling Sharon and reading these words to her from the box office:

(A young child runs down the aisle.) Small Boy: "Come on, Dad, we're gonna be late for Christmas dinner." (The Storyteller walks toward him, and as he moves, we notice he is limping.)

That's one of my favorite instances of "Wow! Thank you, God." That's another thing I'd like to say. I think of creativity as being very close to God, or my perception of God. As Tennessee Williams wrote..."Sometimes -there's God – so quickly!"

Q: Why is theater important in our lives?

A: The theater holds a mirror up to our common humanity. And it's communal. We will never be in the same space in the same way, this way, ever again. That's why it's unique to television and film and even the visual arts, which are mostly fixed and static. The theater combines the best of all those forms. It's been proven (and I don't need a study) that theatergoers are more empathetic. And boy, does the world need that.

I think we are all born creative. As children, we play bank or dress up or Star Wars or Dark Shadows, and somewhere along the way, some of us lose that. Going to a production could spark that impulse we had to play once again. The people who love the theater are closest to their creative side. The people who love the theater are concerned with others. The people who love the theater are lucky. I am so, so lucky.

Sanders knows that the creative spirit that thrives inside Civic Theatre. Civic has used creativity to entertain audiences for ninety-six years; now they're going to need it to ensure they survive another ninety. Because after all, the show...must go on.

40

CAN CREATIVITY GROW REVENUE?

Whether it's an idea for a new product or an innovative way to solve a difficult challenge, every company today needs to embrace creativity if they hope to stay relevant. As we enter an era of creative intensification, companies that are unwilling to foster a creative environment will find it increasingly difficult to compete with companies that do. So how does it work? How do you bring more creativity into a place of business? Can it be used to drive revenue? Absolutely.

To start, it's about being willing to foster an environment where people feel comfortable and are encouraged to openly share ideas and thoughts freely. Leaders within the company must be willing to listen to anyone who wants to share their thoughts. The best leaders understand that a good idea can come from anyone, regardless of their position in the company.

When a leader feels like all the ideas must come from them, they miss a huge opportunity to gain insights into how to innovate from those who are in the best position to know what the company needs to do to keep growing—the employees. Instead, the best leaders will set the stage for innovation to flourish, not by controlling or micromanaging it but by setting the conditions and trusting the process. *"Create the kind of workplace and company culture that will attract great talent. If you hire brilliant people, they will make work feel like play,"* said Sir Richard Branson, who founded the Virgin Group, which today controls more than 400 companies worldwide.

For example, a two-year in-house creativity course at General Electric resulted in a 60% increase in patentable concepts, while creativity training participants at Pittsburgh Plate Glass showed a 300% increase in viable ideas compared with those who didn't take the course. Those are significant increases and worthy of attention. Linda Naiman, founder of Creativity at Work, said, *"For innovation to truly flourish, organizations must create an environment that fosters creativity. They need to bring together multi-talented groups of people who work in close collaboration together — exchanging knowledge, ideas, and shaping the direction of the company's future."*

Richard Florida wrote, *"Ideas are the currency of the new economy." But you have to go all in. For creativity to truly deliver an ROI, everyone in the company has to be on board. You have to be willing to check your ego at the door and embrace a culture where everyone can feel safe to voice their opinions."*

I can't tell you how many times I've been in a room and witnessed someone get humiliated because they had summoned the courage to speak up only to be told, "Well, we've tried that already, and it didn't work!" That employee took a risk to offer a thought, only to be made to feel that their contribution was silly and unworthy of consideration. Creativity won't flourish in a judgmental environment. Before you set up a creative culture, here are some things you will need to implement

- Be willing to entertain different opinions
- Permit people to fail
- Be open to testing new approaches
- Embrace ambiguity
- Get comfortable with being uncomfortable
- Always be curious
- Let go of your ego
- Be authentic with how you interact with everyone
- Show empathy and appreciation
- Give people permission to try untested solutions
- Work on your listening skills
- Be willing to take risks
- Don't feel like you have to have all the ideas
- Openly admit when you are wrong
- Have the courage to hold yourself accountable

Do these things consistently, and I can promise you you'll see an impact. The best part is that once you integrate these items into your culture and do it from a pure place, the benefits are real, and if you do it right, you'll be making more than money; you'll be making an impact.

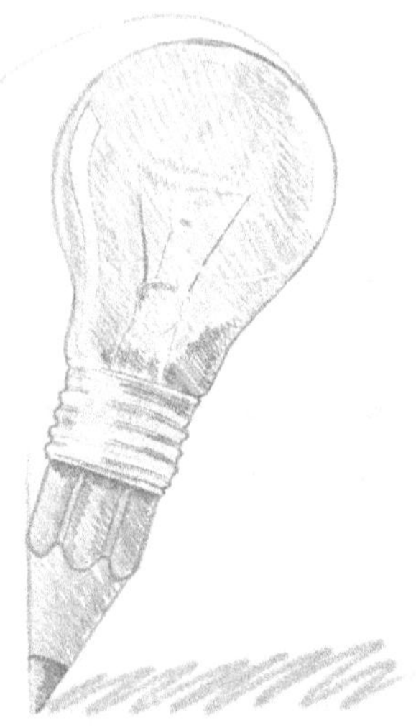

Your ability to adapt to change is the single best indicator for how well you'll embrace unplanned opportunities.

41

LIVE YOUR TRUTH BY EMBRACING YOUR AUTHENTICITY

At some point in your work life, you may find yourself dealing with a situation where you feel like the passion has waned or that you're struggling to find meaning in your career. I can tell you from my own experience that when it happened to me, it was devastating. It led to a bout of anxiety and depression, and I knew that if I hoped to find my way out of the nightmare I was living through, it was going to require some serious soul-searching on my part. The answer to my dilemma came when I realized that I needed to better align myself and my work by embracing authenticity. I had lost my purpose, and the work I was doing felt meaningless.

Cheyenne Bennett, a leadership and talent coach at Compass Point in Bethlehem, PA, who teaches self-awareness, communication, and healthy conflict skills to business leaders, agrees. *"I've done a lot of research on employee engagement, and it's all about the alignment you have between your personal 'why' and your work. If you are doing work that you believe fulfills your life's purpose and you can contribute to your job as your true and best self, then you are just overall happier."*

The more enlightened companies today are also discovering that by nourishing a culture where their employees feel appreciated for the value they bring to the organization, the results can be quite significant. Leaders who understand and practice empathy, vulnerability, creativity, and authenticity with those they lead understand these powerful attractants drive employee engagement, allowing innovation to flourish, which adds to the bottom line.

The days of businesses run by leaders who choose fear over hope, deceptiveness over authenticity, or cynicism over creativity are over. *"Leaders need to model the behavior they want from their employees. If they are vulnerable and honest in the fact that they make mistakes too, then the team can feel the same,"* adds Bennett.

We've all been fed a steady diet in movies and books showing us how uninformed bosses conduct themselves in the workplace. Under this new paradigm, authenticity is not just some new buzzword that you throw onto your company's mission statement and hope it gets adopted. It's an approach that's been gaining serious momentum for years.

While Bennett believes influential leaders do set the tone for the atmosphere inside the business, there's still work that can be done to help those who seek the tools needed to stay engaged. Bennett adds, *"I found that the concept of 'meaningful work' is the biggest predictor of engagement—the degree to which you find your actual work significant, the degree to which your work creates meaning for you in your life, and the degree to which you feel your work makes a positive contribution in the world. What this means is that the more you feel a state of significance or positive meaning in your work, the more you will have an internal commitment to your work and display engagement behaviors."*

These changes will not manifest overnight. You have to commit to putting in the work because it's an ongoing, ever-evolving process. Bennett believes that one of the biggest roadblocks to personal growth is fear and adds, "Fear is easily the biggest one.

Fear of looking stupid. Fear of losing your job. Fear of others around you thinking you're weird. But if we can all agree that this is the way we want to do things, then we are better able to let go of these fears."

We should all strive to find our passion in our profession and work for a company or business that's willing to invest in our overall mental health and well-being. If you currently don't find yourself working for a company that promotes this culture, that's okay. You can still look for ways to live your truth and embrace authenticity. Don't get discouraged by letting the noise of others' opinions drown out your inner voice. The secret to finding happiness at work is to have the courage to become the person you were meant to be. And the best part is, it's never too late.

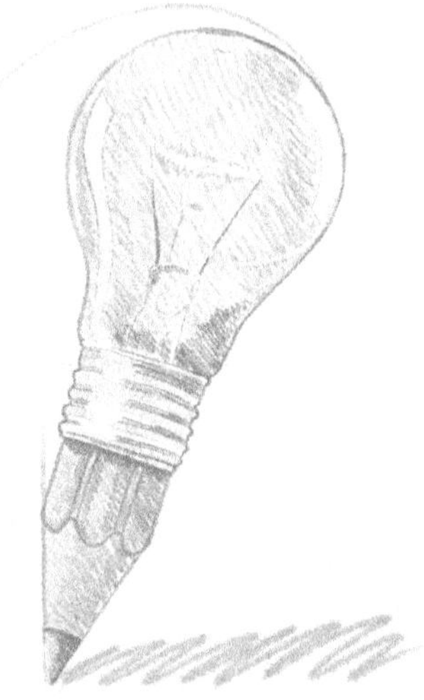

LESSONS LEARNED

Innovation lives on the other side of fear.

42

HOW BUSINESSES CAN INNOVATE USING IMPROVISATION

Leaders often get lost in the maze when it comes to discovering new techniques or processes to help their businesses become more innovative. While improvisational theater is not new, using its principles to train workers to become more creative is, and it holds a vital key to innovation. Improv is not only a thrilling form of entertainment, but it can also help foster collaboration, improve creativity, and increase overall communication within an organization. The very skills needed to do improv on the stage are the same ones that can help people succeed in the workplace.

Dan Maher has witnessed the power improv can have on a person's life. Dan is a writer, director, and the creator of the improv class curriculum at ArtsQuest. He's studied improv at the famed Upright Citizens Brigade, an American improvisational theater and training center in New York City founded by Matt Besser, Amy Poehler, Ian Roberts, and Matt Walsh.

"Improv is an art form that doesn't work without risk. Because for it to work properly, you have to trust those you're performing with to construct the story or scene," Maher says. Businesses today have become more open to the idea of fostering creativity inside their companies but might not understand how to implement the necessary training to get the most from those initiatives. Setting up a creative environment involves more than just creating a quiet room with some bean bag chairs and a foosball table. It takes consistent effort, commitment and strong leadership. Learning how to do improv helps foster trust, encourages risk, and sets up the conditions for people to seek common ground when working together.

It doesn't matter if you are performing in front of a theater audience or presenting to a new client. The ability to improvise in both scenarios is relevant. One of the most significant tenets of improv is known as "yes, and…" It works like this: no matter what your improv partner presents to you, instead of negating it or disagreeing with it, your job is to say, "Yes, and…" That's what helps drive the idea and the collaboration within a scene. You take what your partner presents, and you add to it. They, in turn, do the same thing back to you. That simple yet effective approach should be a staple in every meeting in every company in America: the courage to take a coworker's thought or idea and apply "yes, and…" to it and see where it leads.

Viola Spolin, an accomplished actress, educator, director and author during the early part of the last century, created something called "theater games," a system of actor training that used games she devised to teach the formal rules of the theater. *"Play touches and stimulates vitality, awakening the whole person — mind, body, intelligence, and creativity. The techniques of the theater are the techniques of communication,"* Spolin said. Maher agrees and adds, *"Improv helps me get back in touch with my creativity. It helps me make sense of the chaos and encourages my sense of play, which I think is missing in a lot of people's lives. What's important to me is the pursuit of the craft. I want to do this thing well, and I want to share it with others, and if I can do that for the rest of my life, I know I'll be happy."*

181

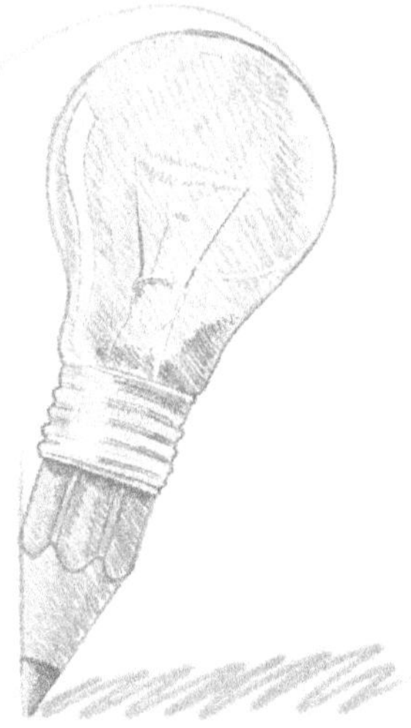

LESSONS LEARNED

You will always learn more from a failure than you will from a success.

43

THE CURE FOR ADVERPANICKING

I'm amazed at what passes for advertising anymore. When done well, advertising is an ongoing dialog with your customers as well as an invitation to attract new ones. Cramming ads with store hours, address, number of years in business, directions to your location, photos of your kids, an inventory of every item in the store, and a bunch of vendor logos, along with other irrelevant information, is a term I call "adverpanicking."

Yet day after day, week after week, there it is, on full display. These ads scream at me from every direction to try this new service, buy this car, come to our show, eat here because we're open late, buy here because we're family-owned, blah, blah, blah. They all suffer from the same problem. All these ads answer questions that no one is asking. Those answers don't become important until after a customer is convinced you have a product or service that they are interested in possessing.

You may be wondering at this point what would happen during an economic downturn. One could argue, *"Hey, I can't afford to get creative with my brand right now; I just need customers."* Truthfully, the best time for a business to steal market share is when everyone else is cutting back. The irony is this: had you been creative with your brand before the economy went south, even a down market wouldn't have knocked you too far off of center. You'd feel it, but stealing market share would already be happening. The only way to attract customers in any economy is to have a compelling message...the type of message that allows for consumer participation in your brand story, where consumers can identify with your company's ethos. Unfortunately, that has nothing to do with your store hours or the number of years in business. The purpose of advertising goes far beyond the circulation of information. When done right, it's an opportunity to create lasting brand loyalty—something every business covets.

Consider this: Apple Computer doesn't sell electronics; they sell innovation. Harley-Davidson doesn't sell motorcycles; they sell freedom. Corona does not sell beer; they sell relaxation. These brands spend a lot of money to own these emotions. The key to creating a meaningful dialog is knowing who you are and what you're selling. If I owned a mattress store, I would not sell the mattresses in my advertising; I would sell the prospect and benefits of a good night's sleep.

If you're connecting to your audience emotionally and the product or service you offer is of high quality, you won't have trouble keeping or attracting customers. With five thousand messages attacking the average consumer daily, you shouldn't be surprised if the world isn't beating a path to your door. David Ogilvy once said, *"You can't bore people into buying your product."* Amen to that. So what's it going to be? Make the burst in your ads a different color and hope that works? How about taking a good, hard look at your message and asking yourself if you're saying anything worthwhile or just adding to the noise? You don't need to spend the kind of money that Apple Computer spends to cut through the clutter, but you do have to be willing to sing in your voice. Tell the market a story that's uniquely yours and do it consistently and compellingly, and you'll have all the customers you'll ever need. Does your advertising suffer from adverpanic?

You just read the cure.

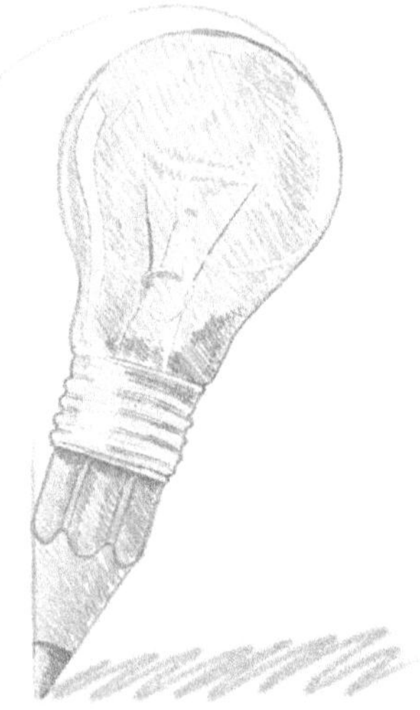

L E S S O N S
LEARNED

Personal media preference should never dictate your marketing strategy.

44

GUITAR BUILDER HITS ALL THE RIGHT NOTES

Custom guitar builder Matt Artinger is an excellent example of what can happen when your passion meets your purpose. Growing up in Allentown, he loved to build things. However, once he picked up his first guitar and started learning how to play it, he was hooked.

"I knew from a young age that building guitars would become my career. I started playing guitar at around age twelve, and from that moment on, I was more interested in what made the guitar work than actually learning how to play it," Artinger says. During his high school years, he apprenticed with master cabinetmaker John Angelino of Angelino's Custom Cabinets in Fogelsville. Soon after, he started Artinger Custom Guitars in Emmaus.

While Artinger knew at an early age what he wanted to do for a career, not everyone is that lucky. The Greek philosopher Socrates offered this: *"At the intersection where your gifts, talents, and abilities meet a human need, therein you will discover your purpose."* How are young kids today going to be able to find their talents and purpose at an early age if there are no substantial opportunities to discover them? When I attended Harrison-Morton Junior High in the mid-'70s, I remember attending woodshop, print, machine, and electrical classes. Those shop classes were an excellent opportunity to get exposed to a trade or skill that I would not typically have the chance to experience. In fact, those classes helped inform my decision to attend Lehigh County Technical Institute in 1980.

Artinger agrees. *"Schools have moved away from some of the more hands-on programs that existed when I went to school. I fondly remember woodshop and graphic arts as some of my favorite classes."* After high school, he attended the prestigious Red Wing Technical College in Red Wing, Minnesota, where he honed his craft in their premier guitar-making program. Artinger channeled his talents and shaped them into a career as one of the most sought-after builders of custom guitars in our area. *"There is a huge difference between something mass-produced and something custom-made. Although I'm not knocking mass-produced instruments, it's just that when you're working one-on-one in a client/artist relationship, every single detail of the guitar build gets scrutinized. We spend much more time on those details to get them exactly right every time,"* he adds. How much more impactful would our current educational model be if every child received the level of attention that Matt describes in his guitar-making process?

"It's very true that art and music programs are the targets of budget cuts in schools, and I think that's a shame. I don't think I would have evolved into who I am without them, and hopefully, there are still creative outlets in schools for kids to get the opportunity to

stretch their wings and explore their artistic sides," he adds. Artingerwas fortunate that he found outlets in school for his talents, which helped him hone his skills and start his business at the age of nineteen. Future job opportunities will depend on how well we help the next generation discover their unique talents and show them how their abilities can provide a rewarding and fulfilling career.

**Success is about growing
yourself. Leadership is
about growing others.**

45

HOW THE PANDEMIC DROVE CREATIVITY AND INNOVATION

Innovation is a messy business. Most companies already know that they need it to survive; many keep plugging along, hoping that the challenges they face will solve themselves. That's not a sustainable strategy. Another challenge with innovation is that it doesn't always follow a predictable pattern, making it hard to replicate. It's also inherently risky in that the results are often hard to track.

In 2020, we all got to experience what can happen when your world suddenly gets turned upside down. The pandemic forced all of us out of our comfort zones and required us to think differently. Both people and businesses had to rapidly deploy new approaches and strategies while trying to maintain a sense of normalcy, and the years since then were anything but normal. New York Times best-selling author Steven Johnson, who penned the book Where Good Ideas Come From, wrote, *"If you look at history, innovation doesn't come from giving people incentives; it comes from creating environments where their ideas can connect."* Whenever you find yourself facing a challenge where you need to reinvent yourself or the way you do business, you can expect to feel a certain amount of anxiety and frustration. Interestingly, those are the same ingredients needed to spark a creative mindset, which is what you'll need to solve a challenge when the odds are stacked against you.

Visionary leaders know that the solution to these difficult times can often be found by setting up an environment for people to feel comfortable sharing new ideas. Sir Richard Branson, no stranger to creativity and innovation, having started more than 400 companies worldwide, said, *"Innovation happens when people are given the freedom to ask questions and the resources and power to find the answers."* For any idea to have a chance of surviving, a couple of steps need to happen. First, somebody needs to have the courage to share the idea or thought. Second, there needs to be a clearly defined path on how to bring the idea to life. Third, and probably most important, the team needs to understand that there's a chance the idea may not work.

That last step is essential because if the concept fails to generate a result—and remember, most don't—the person who originated the idea should not be made to feel marginalized. The worst thing any leader can do in that situation is to stigmatize a mistake. That's the best way to shut down any future innovation. Instead, you regroup, you learn from it, and you move on.

David Kidder, CEO of Bionic, a company that works with other companies to unlock growth mindsets, agrees. *"You can't say to someone, 'I want you to think differently, work differently, behave differently—and then say, 'Go back to your desk.' It doesn't square with the idea that we want you to create growth. As founders and as leaders, we need to alter people's environments to change the way people think and create."* British

Soap Company LUSH created 30-Second Soap, a self-timing soap designed to dissolve away after thirty seconds of vigorous use. The idea is that the soap tells you how long you should wash your hands. Rather brilliant when you think about it, and yet it took the pandemic to bring this idea into the light. So simple, yet so perfect in every way.

Einstein captured the essence of innovation perfectly in this quote: *"Innovation is not the product of rational thought, even though the final product is tied to a logical structure."* Transformative ideas come in all shapes and sizes and often through trial and error.

I hope that the innovation the pandemic inspired continues. My wish is that even though 2020 was not what any of us ever expected could happen, you were able to use the downtime to your advantage by adopting new approaches and strategies for both your business and personal lives. After all, life isn't going to get any easier, but your ability to move through adversity when it arrives is the one guaranteed way to drive real change and innovation.

L E S S O N S
LEARNED

The greatest journey you'll ever take is the one that leads you to your authentic self.

46

APPRECIATING THOSE WHO WORK OUTSIDE THE LIMELIGHT

Did you ever stop to consider the sheer number of people who get up every day and do their jobs without any fanfare or significant recognition? You may even be one of them. Very few of us know what it feels like to run a Fortune 100 company, make decisions that can affect millions of people, or have a platform as a social media influencer with millions of followers on TikTok or Instagram.

I remember the TV show Dirty Jobs where the host, Mike Rowe, toured the U.S. to find the dirtiest jobs people do to earn their living. The show brilliantly revealed that many incredibly dedicated and passionate people love their dirty jobs. The program profiled ordinary people doing extraordinary things to keep our country moving forward. It gave the country insight into those who work outside the limelight. Author David Zweig wrote a fascinating book titled Invisibles: The Power of Anonymous Work in an Age of Relentless Self-

Promotion, said, *"Invisibles are in all walks of life. What binds them is their approach—deriving satisfaction from the value of their work, not the volume of their praise,"* to which he added, *"We might think that the person at the head of the boardroom table is the one with all the responsibility. Still, it's often someone unknown to the public who bears much of the weight."*

Have you ever worked at a company where you felt anonymous and unappreciated? If you have, then you know how demoralizing it can be. Yet one of the easiest ways to let someone know you respect their contributions is to acknowledge that you see them. Telling someone you "see" them lets them know on a deeper level that you recognize that they matter. Unfortunately, many leaders don't understand this straightforward, uncomplicated approach.

Telling employees you appreciate them is still a great way to honor their role in the business. Another one is paying them a wage that reflects that appreciation. The two are not mutually exclusive. If the era of the great resignation showed us anything, it's that people want more than just a paycheck for their work.

Eric Mosley, CEO and co-founder of Workhuman®, a company that helps the world's leading brands build cultures that leverage the power of connection, said, *"People achieve their fullest potential when they feel appreciated, connected, and empowered to be who they are in their work. People want purpose, meaning, and gratitude. Purpose is shared, meaning is personal, and gratitude is the great connector."*

**Here are some people I think are
worthy of serious appreciation:**

To the bus drivers who ensure their riders get where they need to go safely and on time. I see you. To the healthcare workers, nurses, home health aides, nursing assistants, and janitorial staff on the front lines fighting to keep us healthy while putting their health at risk, I see you.

To the teachers who show up every day and do everything they know to inspire their students, I see you. To the mechanics who keep our cars and airplanes running, the welders who build our cities, and the farmers who grow and cultivate our food supply. From the restaurant industry professionals working long hours to the volunteer crossing guards who ensure that children safely cross the street, I see you.

Bank tellers, daycare professionals, librarians, civil servants, postal workers, I see all of you, and I'm grateful for you. Every single one of those jobs is crucial to our success as a nation. It's not difficult to find someone in your world who shows up consistently and does their work at a high level without any self-aggrandizement. After all, the people who don't go looking for appreciation are the ones who deserve it the most.

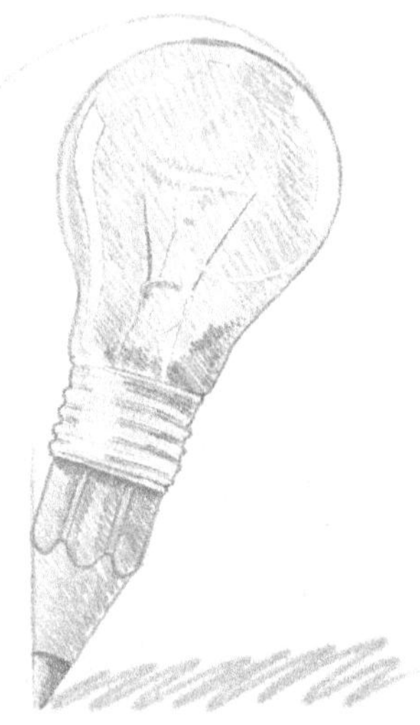

L E S S O N S
LEARNED

Good leaders understand the importance of failing your way to success, not shrinking your way to greatness.

47

NAVIGATING THE CHALLENGES OF A CAREER CHANGE

Seems like every January, many of us arrive at the special time of the year where we grow introspective and take a hard look at the state of our lives. It could be financial, personal, or professional. One of the topics that always leaps to the fore for many people is their current employment situation. Deciding whether or not you're ready to try a career pivot and begin the search for a new challenge is often a critical first step.Even after the decision is made to explore a change, many are reluctant over how to go about doing it.

Barbara Berger, owner/founder of Career Wellness Partners, a career coaching and employee career management firm understands these challenges very well. *"Work is an expression of who we are. At best, work is an extension of our genuine selves. At worst, it is a fake costume we put on every day that can become so heavy that the stress ripples out to all areas of our lives,"* Berger cautions. She started Career Wellness Partners because she was always fascinated by people's career stories, and since she worked as a hiring manager who interviewed candidates all day, it fueled her curiosity about how wellness at work affects overall welfare. She understood the hiring side, but she wanted to immerse herself in helping people align themselves with their next career steps. *"I provide the motivation, support, and accountability for taking those crucial next steps. I also evaluate the term 'career' and create their definition of career wellness. If 'career' to someone means caring for loved ones or volunteer work and to another it means being a CEO or anything in between, I can help them get clear on defining what provides meaningful contribution and value against their scale, accepting that, and moving from there,"* she adds.

The reasons people often switch jobs can be varied' however, most people who voluntarily leave companies don't necessarily leave because of money. A recent Gallup poll found that 32% leave for career advancement/promotional opportunities. To Berger, employee retention not only saves the company time and money, but employees who are engaged are more productive and happier.

"When companies are committed to helping employees understand their strengths and motivators and offer opportunities like job shadowing or project participation outside of the employee's normal scope, it shows commitment to employee career development, and it has lasting effects," she stresses. British entrepreneur and Virgin Atlantic CEO Richard Branson agrees. *"Train people well enough so they can leave, treat them well enough so they don't want to."* So, while every year January seems to struggle out of the gate, things will pick up steam as people come back from holiday time off and begin their year in earnest. Hiring managers often look for exact fits for positions, which can make it challenging for career changers.

The length of a job search could be two weeks, or it could be a year or more. There are many factors to consider, including how proactive the job seeker is, how significant the shift is, what their level of seniority is, and more.

Berger advises career changers to be realistic about their timeline and financial reserves. Career transition coaches understand the ebbs and flows of a job search, and they can be vital in helping you narrow your search criteria and keeping you positive and focused if things don't go as planned.

With unemployment holding steady at 3.7%, employers are going to have to find more creative ways to stop their best employees from seeking greener pastures. For employers, just throwing money at the problem might not prove to be the best option. Employers need to monitor and analyze their employee retention strategies every quarter to stay competitive with market salaries, benefits, workplace cultures, and office perks

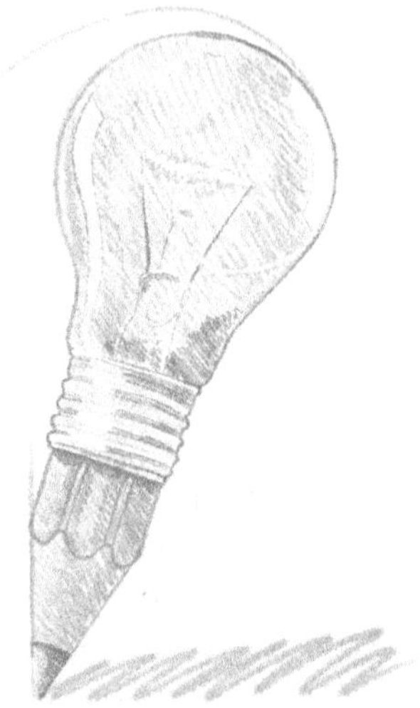

L E S S O N S
LEARNED

You don't need a big budget to discover a big idea.

48

THE CREATIVITY CRISIS

Growing up, I spent a great deal of time wondering about the career path I would choose to earn my living. The challenge was choosing a career where I could get paid doing something I loved. Easier said than done, right? However, I always felt a strong pull toward the more creative aspects of life, so a career where creativity is needed made the most sense. One thing I wish I knew before starting my career was the inherent creative bias that I would experience in the business world because I live out of the right side of my brain.

Now, compelling new research proves that creativity is indeed facing a crisis. In March of this year, a business professor at the University of Illinois at Urbana-Champaign, Jack Goncalo, and his colleagues released their study proving that most people harbor a strong aversion to creators and creative types.

The study, conducted over ten years, showed that creativity is viewed by many as 'noxious' and 'disruptive.' Goncalo's other findings revealed that innovative thought often gets outrightly rejected because of its power to intensify feelings of uncertainty. Ironic when you consider that you won't develop transformative ideas without vast amounts of uncertainty, ambiguity, and risk. Begging the conundrum: How do you expect to grow your business if you're unwilling to disrupt the status quo? The short answer is you can't. There will never be enough statistics to prove value when it's in question, but good ideas and creativity nullify the stats; they create buzz, energy, and excitement. Creativity represents change, and if change makes you uncomfortable, how do you expect to make decisions that will move your business forward?

Change is the only thing constant in business, so why all the discomfort? Jennifer Mueller, an expert in creativity science and a professor of management at the University of San Diego, said, *"We have an implicit belief the status quo is safe, novel ideas have almost no upside for a middle manager — almost none. The goal of a middle manager is meeting metrics of an existing paradigm."* Best-selling author and creativity expert Edward de Bono agrees, *"Most executives, many scientists, and almost all business school graduates believe that if you analyze the data, it will give you new ideas. Unfortunately, this belief is wrong."* He also believes that *"There is no doubt that creativity is the most important human resource of all. Without creativity, there would be no progress, as we would forever repeat the same patterns."*

While the research I referenced here may indicate an inherent bias towards creative individuals, there is still hope. To all the creative people working through difficult situations, I say, keep pushing, keep grinding, and embrace your wonderment. Keep showing up and doing good work. You represent one of the best chances a company or a society has to evolve and grow due to your unique ability to use your imagination, curiosity, and open-mindedness for the greater good. Keep bringing your intrinsic motivation to get things done, as I would argue that creative skills are needed now more than ever. As I look back on my chosen career path, I remain optimistic. I have learned that anything in life worth doing is going to contain its fair share of struggles and obstacles. My creativity has served as both a blessing and a curse. There were times throughout my career when my imagination was celebrated, and other times not so much.

In retrospect, I wouldn't change a thing as we are all the total of our experiences. You need failure and success to grow into your best version. I do know this; the struggle IS the journey because difficult roads are the ones that lead to the most rewarding destinations.

Acknowledgements:

First and foremost, I want to thank my incredible wife, Kelly Childs Forte, for her unwavering encouragement and support in getting Childs Play out into the world. You can do great things when you have someone who believes in you. Thank you, Kelly. I love you very much. To my children, Autumn, Willow, and Zane, thank you for the absolute privilege of being your father and watching you grow into the amazing adults you are today. To my sister, Tracy, who had to deal with more than her share of my stupidity while growing up, thank you for being so understanding, I love you. To my parents, Nancy and Leroy, I carry your loving memories in my heart; to my grandmother, Mary, you kept me stocked with fresh coloring books and crayons when I was young and always encouraged my artistic side. To my brother from another mother, my cousin, Mike Lipovsky, you were always there for me. To all my teachers at the Herbst School, Mrs. Almeida, Mrs. Lobus, Mrs. Wittenbrader, Mrs. Bachman, and especially Mr. Novak, for encouraging my sense of wonder and imagination. To Sarah Sterner-Hausknecht and Nichole Smith, for your artistic contributions and for being such fantastic people to work with all these years. To Debbie Burke for your editing expertise, Mary Lengle for your publishing advice and infectious positivity, Luca and Catarina Raposa for accepting me into your lives, and Rob Dougherty for the invaluable advice regarding this book. To the friends who keep me grounded, Jeff Olaf, Chris Ortman, Jason Wilson, and Mike Mannicci, thank you, boys. To my former and current students at LCTI, you inspire me every day, and I thank you for showing up for the process and keep dreaming big. To my mentors, Bruce Silvernell, Dan Ross, John Hayes, Myron Barnstone, Pat Maley, and Darryl Schellhamer: you have all guided and supported me in a multitude of ways over the years. I'm forever grateful for the countless hours of communication and your mentorship. To author Hugh MacLeod for your inspirational book on creativity, Ignore Everybody, which was a huge inspiration and catalyst for me wanting to write Childs Play. Cheers, Hugh. I also want to thank my fellow co-workers at Graphic Sign Systems/ Spandex USA, The Morning Call Newspaper, Adams Outdoor Advertising, RM Squared/Forge Marketing Communications, Trifecta Technologies, Kitchen Magic, and Lehigh Career and Technical Institute. Without you, this book would not exist. I'd like to thank the rest of my family and friends who have supported me through this endeavor. You know who you are.

About the author:

William Childs, has spent forty years in pursuit of his craft in the filed of advertising and marketing, but his true love has always been creativity. *"Growing up, when you're a child, you are at the height of your creative and imaginative powers. Then, as you grow and age, it gets slowly depleted and squandered, sometimes never to found or used again. "We don't grow into our creativity; we get educated out of it,"* said, Sir Ken Robinson.

Through real-world examples and insights over a 40-year career, Childs knows how to get people to tap into what's already inside them and put it to use.

Childs is an accomplished creative leader with a history of delivering award-winning campaigns and implementing creative cultures. He's relentlessly dedicated to the skillful and creative translation of strategic business objectives into revenue-generating campaigns. Known as a collaborative mentor and champion of fearless creativity who celebrates and develops team talent.

Childs has worked as a paste up artist, layout artist, sign maker, designer, art director, copywriter, newspaper and magazine columnist, lecturer, salesperson, art director, marketing director, podcaster, creative director, and is currently an Advertising Design Instructor at LCTI in Schnecksville, PA. All the roles Childs has performed over the years, required large amounts of creativity to excel at a high level. It's through these positions that Childs was able to work out many of the concepts that appear in this book.

Childs is an accomplished public speaker and lecturer.
Childs speaks extensively at colleges and universities on the topics covered in Childs Play.
He can be reached at: wpchilds1@rcn.com.

CHILDS PLAY

"If you want to be creative,
stay in part a child,
with the creativity and
invention that characterizes
children before they are
deformed by adult society."

- Jean Piaget